BART SIMPSON'S

Guide to Life

Helped into print by M~~att Groening~~

HarperCollins*Pu*

D0228735

Dedicated to the memory of Snowball I:
Whenever we hear a cat yowling at 3 A.M., whenever we
slip on a slimy hairball, whenever we inhale the tart aroma
of a neglected cat box, we think of you.

This edition specially produced in 1997
for The Book People Ltd, Catteshall Manor,
Catteshall Lane, Godalming, SURREY GU7 1UU

Published by HarperCollins*Publishers* 1996
77–85 Fulham Palace Road, London W6 8JB
9 8

First published in the USA by HarperCollins Publishers Inc. 1993

A catalogue record for this book is
available from the British Library

ISBN 0 583 33168 8

Printed and bound in Great Britain by
Caledonian International Book Manufacturing Ltd, Glasgow

Concepts/Art Direction: MILI SMYTHE
Supreme Scrivener: JAMIE ANGELL
Logistical Overlord: DOUG WHALEY
Design: PETER ALEXANDER, DOUG WHALEY
Computer Whiz: DANIEL AMANTE
Contributing Writers: PETER ALEXANDER, JAMIE ANGELL, TED BROCK,
EILEEN CAMPION, MAX FRANKE, JIM JENSEN, BARBARA MCADAMS,
BILL MORRISON, MILI SMYTHE, MARY TRAINOR, DOUG WHALEY
Research Boy: JIM JENSEN
Artists: BILL MORRISON, DALE HENDRICKSON, JOHN ADAM
Legal Guardian: SUSAN GRODE
Editor: WENDY WOLF
Film Separations: GRAPHICS PLUS
Special Thanks to Christina Simonds and the L.A. Public Library System

Hello there, friend, and welcome to *Bart Simpson's Guide to Life*. If you didn't swipe this book,* and it wasn't a gift, then we here at the Bart Simpson Foundation for Personal Enrichment must assume that you actually paid money for this merchandise. Therefore we must assume that you are a concerned and sensitive individual seeking truth and understanding, one who cares deeply about the environment and his or her fellow human beings, one who is eager to embark on the long but worthwhile journey to enlightenment.

Welcome to Suckersville, man.

* To the thieving dog who did swipe this book. I know who you are. I know where you live, and I will hunt you down and kill you. Maybe not this week, maybe not next week. But someday, when you least expect it . . . you're dead meat, man.

To discover the secret of the meaning of life. turn to page 144...

1

School

FORGERY!

Okay, listen up, man! We all know that kids have to do tons of stuff that reall[y] stinks. But only one thing is so bad, so vile, so unfair, so downright *awful,* they had to pass a *law* to make us do it. That's right, *school.* Twelve years of hard time. Tot[e] that book! Lift those grades! Learn to read! You can't get away! ...Or *can* you[?]

By mastering one simple skill, you can slip through the clutches of the law *an[d]* take the breaks you deserve. The art of forging signatures–smoothly, cleanly, an[d] repeatedly–will let *you* live your life the way *you* see fit. Here are a few crucial documents you'll use again and again. Take these examples, memorize 'em, use 'em, and practice, practice, *practice*, man!

THE NEVER FAIL SICK EXCUSE

Please excuse _____ for
(your name here)
missing school the past two days. He/she was
suffering from amnesia and forgot to go to school.
He/she is much better now, thank you. Please never
mention this to anyone, as it may trigger a relapse.

Sincerely,

_____
(your parent's signature)

THE GET-OUT-OF-GYM ROUTINE

_____
(your name here)
injured his/her back carrying me
across a puddle. He/she must not
do anything that even sounds like
exercise. Ever. Or we will sue you
for everything you've got.

Sincerely,

_____
(your parent's signature)

THE PERFECT PROGRESS REPORT

Dear Mr. and/or Mrs. _____ (your last name here),

I am writing to let you know how well _____ (your name here) is doing in my class. We all think she/he's totally cool and hope she/he'll never change. How did she/he learn to whistle like that?

Someday I might write to tell you how horrible _____ (your name here) is, but I am a paranoid schizophrenic, so please ignore me then, or I might kill you.

Sincerely,

_____ (your teacher's signature)

THE ULTIMATE HALL PASS

_____ (your name here) is on an emergency mission, resurfacing my hairpiece. Do not detain her/him for one second more, or I will assign you detention for the rest of the year.

Sincerely,

_____ (your principal's signature)

By now, you can see the power and the freedom that is yours to command, man. So start a-forgin' with your folks' signatures, then learn your teachers' (good for one year and worth it), and your principal's (good for your entire stay at that school). Proof that the pen *can* be mightier than the sword!

Last-Minute

SHOW &

On your way out the door before you realize it's Show & Tell day? Here are some official Bart-tested crowd pleasers guaranteed to pull you through in a pinch. Old rule of thumb — if you can't dazzle 'em with brilliance, baffle 'em with bull. Remember — always keep a straight face. And if all else fails... gross 'em out!

3. Potato chips in the shape of celebrities (Richard Nixon is a sure-fire crowd pleaser.)

4. Stitches (Always impressive, be creative in explaining how they got there.)

AROUND THE HOUSE
1. Scars (Will do in a pinch; make up a good story.)

2. Granny's dentures (squirmifying!)

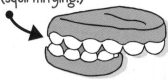

5. Baby teeth (Wait 'til they fall out before taking.)

6. The baby (Wait 'til Mom's not looking before taking.)

6

More
SHOW & TELL
ideas

17. The DO NOT REMOVE label torn from the end of your mattress

18. Your parents' old love letters (You know where they are. Or ask your mom when she's feeling sentimental to show you, so you'll know where they are in the future.)

19. Rotten milk (Pass it around to smell.)

HAVE YOU SEEN ME?

FROM THE GARDEN

20. Rotten fruit or vegetables (preferably with mold)

21. Tomato worms

22. Stinkbugs

23. Praying mantis (Get 2 and watch them fight—the winner will eat the loser!)

24. Larvae of any kind

25. Earthworms (Bring plenty to share!)

26. Decomposed pets (Dig them up for a real horror show.)

27. Garden slugs (You can race 'em!)

FROM THE NEIGHBORHOOD

28. Lingerie mail-order catalogs

DEAr MARGE,
Can you loan
me ten bucks?
x x x
Homer
P.S. I love you.

WHEN ALL ELSE FAILS

32. Your invisible friend

29. Your neighbor's garbage
(Garbology is now a legal law
enforcement procedure.)

30. NO TRESPASSING signs

31. Dirt (Add water to
make mud!)

YOUR PLAYFUL GUIDE TO
PLAYGROUND
PLAYMATES

PLAYGROUND PLAYMATE	PERSONALITY TRAITS	FAVORITE PLAYTIME ACTIVITY	MOST OVERHEARD REMARK	PROBABL FUTURE PROFESSIO
 THE WHINY CRYBABY	Passive-aggressive	Running to the nurse's office	"OW! That hurt! I'm telling!!!"	Personal Injury Attorney
 LITTLE MISS BACK STABBER	Aggressive-aggressive	Hanging out in the girls' bathroom	"I know something you don't know!"	Gossip Columnist
 THE BIG BULLY	Massive-aggressive	Lynchings, beatings	Grunting	Security Guard

AYGROUND PLAYMATE	PERSONALITY TRAITS	FAVORITE PLAYTIME ACTIVITY	MOST OVERHEARD REMARK	PROBABLE FUTURE PROFESSION
 HE LONE PSYCHO	Reclusive-aggressive	Picking stucco off the walls	"Leave me alone."	U.S. Postal Employee
 MR. KNOW-IT-ALL	Massive-abrasive	Sneering at others	"Your stupidity never ceases to amaze me."	Critic
 THE TTENTION SEEKER	Effusive-delusive	Yowling, shrieking, fainting, laughing hysterically, brooding	"Look at me! Look at me! LOOK AT MEEEEE!"	Actor
 MR. BLEND-IN	None whatsoever	None whatsoever	None whatsoever	Data Processor

11

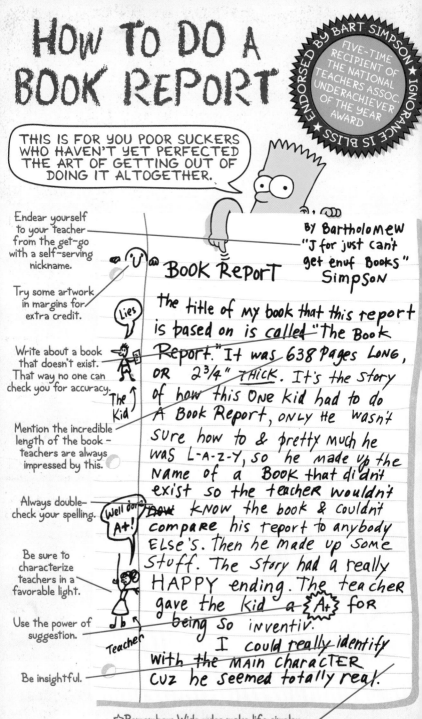

We cannot be responsible for any injury or legal repercussions resulting from the following techniques. Only certified advanced practitioners of underachievement should attempt the following!

- Fake an illness severe enough to prevent you from writing.

- Negotiate – offer to clean the hamster cages in lieu of turning in a report.

- Get your library privileges revoked.

- Start a classroom revolt.

- File a class action lawsuit against your teacher.

- Go "blind."

- Pretend you have converted to a religion that forbids reading of any kind.

I would recomend this Book to anybody, except it May be too intellectual for most grade SCHOOLeRs And even high school kids.

In cunclusion, I'd SAY this was a great Book. It taught me one of Life's most importanT lessons: if YOU'Re GONNA cheat, cheat whole-heartedly. Lastly, I would like to say that if ONLY moRE people would Stay home AnD Read, we'd have 56% less Crime in America today.

Thank You.

And have a lovely day!

There's A Dog in the Book too

If you're in a pinch for filler, add an endorsement.

Reinforce the high-brow aspects of the book.

Use big words generously.

Always include a moral.

Set it up for the grand finale.

Include statistics wherever possible.

Patriotism will almost definitely improve your score!

Be grateful. Teachers like to think you appreciate the torture they put you through.

End on a positive note.

☆Bonus Tip: Double-space your report for maximum impact! (Not shown here.)

13

Bart's Handy-Dandy Guide to...

Cheating

Uh-oh! A surprise quiz popped on you at the last minute? Did you suddenly realize that dreaded history test is TODAY? Has your apathy suddenly turned into terror? Fear not! Just follow my easy-to-use, Handy-Dandy Cheating Guide and your fears will melt away. Take it from a pro, man: Good cheaters aren't born—they're made. Just practice these techniques and you'll be getting C's instead of F's in no time! But if anyone asks, you didn't hear it from me, man!

TIP: IT MAY BE EASIER TO ACTUALLY LEARN THAN TO TRY AND FOLLOW THESE RULES.

Seating

As in real estate, the most important three words are: location, location, location. DON'T sit near the teacher! That's obvious. Here are a few more specifics. Use existing cover—sit behind someone with really big hair. Don't sit near any known snitches. Always try to be near a smart person, but if that fails, sit near a cool person who won't mind if you bug 'em for answers. Cooperate with others—it's easier to cheat that way and you can always shift the blame.

Using Signals

Work these out beforehand with a partner. They'll prove invaluable again and again!

TRUE OR FALSE: With one hand, signal the number of the question by holding up fingers, and then with the other, hold your pencil pointing up for true or sideways for false.

MULTIPLE CHOICE: Hold your pencil with the point straight up for A, to the right for B, straight down for C, to the left for D, and break pencil in half and bury your face in your hands when you realize neither of you know the answer.

True

False

A.

B.

C.

D.

Going It Alone

Can't get anyone else interested? It's OK. Here are a few tips that can save your butt.

Crib Notes

Invaluable if you have the time. Before class, get your book (or a knowledgeable friend), sit down, and collect any info you think you will need. Then write on your shoes, wrists, forearms, cap brim, eraser, undershirt, socks, pant legs, etc.

Cheat Sheets

Same principle as Crib Notes, only you write all your info on a piece of paper and hide it up your sleeve or in your fly or someplace that won't be obvious when you read it.

Pencil Drop

Drop your pencil or paper and sneak a peek at other kids' papers when you bend down to pick it up.

A Trip to the Sharpener

Use this valuable time to pick up information you can't get from the dummies directly surrounding your desk.

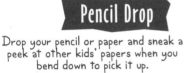

Some Expert Tips

Make smart friends
•
Bribe them
•
Call in any favors owed to you
•
Sleep properly the night before — a stiff neck could mean ruin
•
Practice having shifty eyes
•
Don't be obvious
•
Don't be timid
•
Look innocent
•
Be silent
•
Don't shift and squirm
•
Look thoughtful and pensive
•
Don't attract attention
•
Look around
•
Keep your eye on the teacher at all times
•
Pretend that you know the material
•
Don't get caught
•
Don't mention my name if you do

Food

TABLE MANNERS

SMIK!
SMAK!
SMUK!

We all know manners at the table are important. However, some of you readers may be a tad confused when it comes to the finer points of mealtime etiquette. Never fear, my ill-bred friends: the following are some simple guidelines from yours truly, appropriate for any occasion.

ELBOWS ON THE TABLE

This is always acceptable. In fact, in the United States it is considered highly improper to let your elbows leave the table at any time during a meal.

BANZA

Do you still want to know the meaning of life? Turn to page 62...

PASSING

Everybody knows that the shortest distance between two points is a straight line. So I recommend the forward pass. Bonus points if the food makes it into the intended recipient's mouth. (Not recommended for passing hot grease.)

THE PROPER USE OF UTENSILS

Utensils can be useful from time to time. For example, say your little sister is trying to grab a roll off your plate, a fork comes in very handy. Also, spoons make excellent launch pads. And, of course, steak knives are great for flossing after mea

CHEWING

Many of you have probably asked yourselves: "Should I chew with my mouth open or my mouth closed?" This is a question that has plagued humankind for millions of years. All I can tell you is, there are some mysteries of the universe that we may never fully understand. And perhaps it is best left that way, man.

HELPINGS

The goal here is to keep your siblings from getting anything. If you keep your chewing to a minimum and force everything down with lots of carbo-nated water, you can probably ingest 3 to 4 times as much food as a normal human can in the same amount of time. So keep on a-shovelin', man.

DRESS

For casual affairs, a lobster bib will do. For more formal events, some kind of clothes are recommended. And for birthday parties, you are NOT required to wear one of those stupid hats, so don't let 'em make you.

EATING WITH FINGERS

Certain foods should NEVER be eaten with the fingers. Basically, anything you can suck through a straw should not be eaten with fingers. This includes: pudding, creamed corn, rice, stew, lima beans, and gelatin. However, try as we might, our experts were unable to suck steak through straws, so you will have to eat this with your fingers.

ON SLURPING SOUP

In this country, it is considered polite to slurp any food served to you in liquid form. The louder the slurp, the bigger the compliment to your host or hostess.

TALKING WITH YOUR MOUTH FULL

If you want to say something when your mouth is full of food, it's important to make sure that what you say is entertaining (see "Mealtime Topics") and that the other dinner guests can understand you.

I AW ISH UCK!!!

DOH TAW WIH YO MOW FOOH!**

TRANSLATION:
* MY JAW IS STUCK!!!
** DON'T TALK WITH YOUR MOUTH FULL!

MEALTIME TOPICS

Challenge your parents' views about money, morality, and politics. There's nothing more fun than watching an angry per-son try to swallow and yell at the same time.

TOUCHÉ!

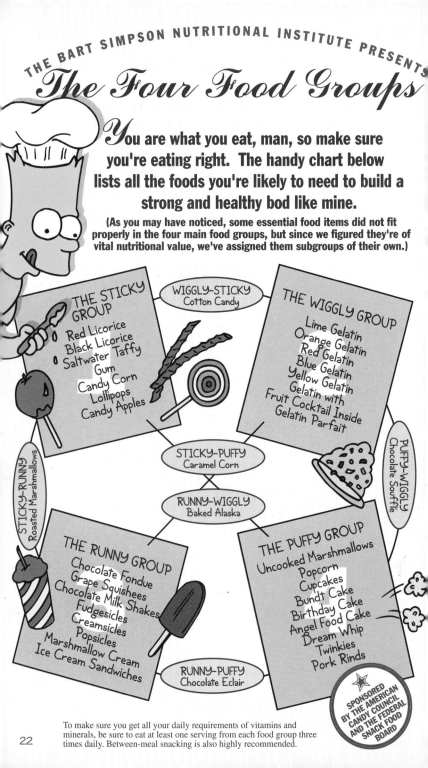

The Four Food Groups

You are what you eat, man, so make sure you're eating right. The handy chart below lists all the foods you're likely to need to build a strong and healthy bod like mine.

(As you may have noticed, some essential food items did not fit properly in the four main food groups, but since we figured they're of vital nutritional value, we've assigned them subgroups of their own.)

WIGGLY-STICKY
Cotton Candy

THE STICKY GROUP
Red Licorice
Black Licorice
Saltwater Taffy
Gum
Candy Corn
Lollipops
Candy Apples

THE WIGGLY GROUP
Lime Gelatin
Orange Gelatin
Red Gelatin
Blue Gelatin
Yellow Gelatin
Gelatin with
Fruit Cocktail Inside
Gelatin Parfait

STICKY-RUNNY
Roasted Marshmallows

PUFFY-WIGGLY
Chocolate Soufflé

STICKY-PUFFY
Caramel Corn

RUNNY-WIGGLY
Baked Alaska

THE RUNNY GROUP
Chocolate Fondue
Grape Squishees
Chocolate Milk Shakes
Fudgesicles
Creamsicles
Popsicles
Marshmallow Cream
Ice Cream Sandwiches

THE PUFFY GROUP
Uncooked Marshmallows
Popcorn
Cupcakes
Bundt Cake
Birthday Cake
Angel Food Cake
Dream Whip
Twinkies
Pork Rinds

RUNNY-PUFFY
Chocolate Eclair

SPONSORED BY THE AMERICAN CANDY COUNCIL AND THE FEDERAL SNACK FOOD BOARD

To make sure you get all your daily requirements of vitamins and minerals, be sure to eat at least one serving from each food group three times daily. Between-meal snacking is also highly recommended.

THE FOOD PYRAMID BARTERING GUIDE

Yo, kids! Not sure of the exact street value of your lunch contents? Been left holding the (empty) bag one too many times? Cut out this handy pocket guide and make sure you never get ripped off again, man!

LEVEL A
- Triple-chocolate ice cream

LEVEL B
- Double-chocolate ice cream
- Chocolate ice cream

LEVEL C
- Chocolate-coated donut
- Chocolate cupcake
- Chocolate pudding

LEVEL D
- Plain cake donut
- Carob-nougat bar
- Fruitcake slice
- Xtra-salty Pork Rinds

LEVEL E
1. Beef jerky stick
2. Pickled egg
3. Pimento loaf sandwich
4. Extra-ripe banana
5. Hot chili-flavored Pork Rinds Lite

LEVEL F
6. Tofutti
7. Date shake
8. Yam gelatin parfait
9. Soy milk (grape-flavored)
10. Prune Whip
11. Unsalted Pork Rinds

LEVEL G
12. Tuna boat
13. Mayonnaise sandwich
14. Kidney pie
15. Can of Clamato
16. Jumbo gherkin
17. Soy milk (plain)
18. Stale bread

LEVEL H
19. Macaroni 'n' Lard
20. Tofu Con Carne
21. Curds 'n' Whey
22. Smelt cakes
23. Limburger croquettes
24. Okra patties
25. Tongue sandwich
26. Pork cracklin's

LET'S MAKE A DEAL, MAN!

To continue on your search for the meaning of life, turn to page 97...

1 A
2 3 B
4 5 6 C
7 8 9 10 D
11 12 13 14 15 E
16 17 18 19 20 21 F
22 23 24 25 26 27 28 G
29 30 31 32 33 34 35 36 H

Each item is worth 2 items in trade from the level below it.
For example: 2 items from LEVEL E
(1 pickled egg + 1 pimento loaf sandwich) could
be traded for 1 item on LEVEL D (1 plain cake donut).

23

Mealtime Fun!

GROSS-OUTS

Compare what other people are eating to gross things their food looks like.

EXAMPLES:

tapioca pudding = fish eyes
spaghetti = bloody worms
soft-boiled eggs = chicken embryos
tuna casserole = cat vomit
sausage links = intestines
liver = liver
kidneys = kidneys

You get the picture.

Stories about car wrecks, broken bones, disfiguring accidents, serial murders, older brothers' girlfriends, granny's dentures, the cat box, maggots, larvae, pupae, worms, rotten eggs, boogers, mucus, B.O., and other wonders of nature are sure to prevent some poor sucker from finishing his meal.

Bodily noises are fun and entertaining. Try one or all of the following:

Hawk a lugee noise with your nose and throat

Fake like you're puking

Play an armpit symphony

Make gagging noises

EATING STRATEGIES

Do you sit at the wrong end of the tab Good items gone before they get to you? Stuck with Brussels sprouts, lima beans an no gravy for your mashed potatoes? Time use strategy to get your fill or to get the swill off your plate, man! Try these metho

TO ACQUIRE FOOD:

FLATTERY— Compliments throw people off their guard. Try something like "Hey, dude, you're looking pretty buff. Mind using those incredible muscles to pass me that last baked potato?" or "Gee, Grandma, your teeth look so real tonight! Mind flashing me those pearly whites as you pass me that gravy boat?"

BRIBES— Desperate times call for desperate measures. Try something like "Hey, Lisa, I'll give you a dollar for that last pork chop," then whisper under your breath, "(in the year 2014)."

You can tell her that part after dinner.

SEE...? FOOD!!!

To the lowlife punk who pinched this book (you know who your are!): Kiss your butt goodbye, man.

24

TO GET RID OF FOOD:

DISTRACTION— "Accidentally" spill your milk. While you're mopping it up, slip your peas into the paper towel and take them to the trash. Or look out the window and exclaim, "Wow! Look at that snail in the window!" While everyone looks, sneak your cauliflower onto your little brother's plate. When they look back, just say, "You missed it. It was green and hairy, but it was moving too fast for you to see it, I guess."

SAYING GRACE— This can also be used as a cover for getting rid of unwanted items. While everyone's heads are bowed and eyes closed, shift the food off your plate and into your lap. Also works well for obtaining desirable food items.

PETS— Dogs will usually eat anything from the table. If you can get something into your lap, the next step of getting it into the dog's mouth shouldn't be difficult at all. For finicky pets, wrap unappetizing food such as spinach in a piece of meat.

GAMES

"SEAFOOD" (The old standard)— Chew up a mouthful of food but don't swallow it. Ask your sister if she would like some "seafood." When she responds in the affirmative, open your mouth and exclaim, "See? Food!!!" People just love this trick.

HIDE AND SEAFOOD— Chew up a mouthful of food and show it to your brother or sister. Then have them try to do the same to you. The first one to get caught by your parents loses.

FOOD AS ART— Some foods cry out to be sculpted. Mashed potatoes (mixed with just about anything) are perfect, but ice cream, oatmeal, and gelatin all work well. Have a contest to see who can make the highest tower. Remember, art knows no bounds.

THE SINGING WINE GLASS (or water glass)— This is a really cool game. Wet your finger and rub it around the edge of a crystal glass and it makes a musical sound. The note will be higher or lower depending on how much liquid is in the glass. Have everyone at the table play, and you'll be conducting a symphony!

THE FIRE BREATHER— Put hot pepper sauce in someone's water when they're not looking. See if they notice.

DUCK 'N' COVER— Food catapults are fun and easy. There's always a spoon and some food at hand. See how far you can fling it... you'll be amazed!

BART!!!

25

FUN FO

Raw bacon makes an excellent face mask.

Asparagus makes your pee turn bright yellow.

Peanuts and almonds are not nuts. A peanut is a legume and an almond is a fruit.

Some hens lay eggs shaped like cucumbers

Wintergreen Lifesavers, when chewed in the dark, give off sparks.

freeze-dried potatoes found in Incan tombs have proved to be edible.

The tomato is native to Peru.

You can feed 24 people with one ostrich egg.

D FACTS

To know and tell!

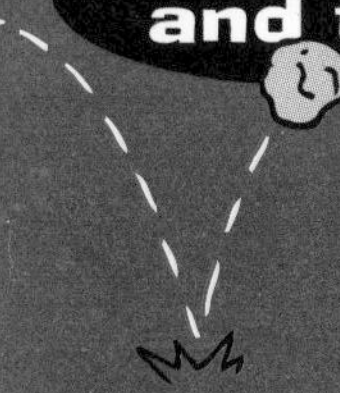

Bubble gum contains rubber.

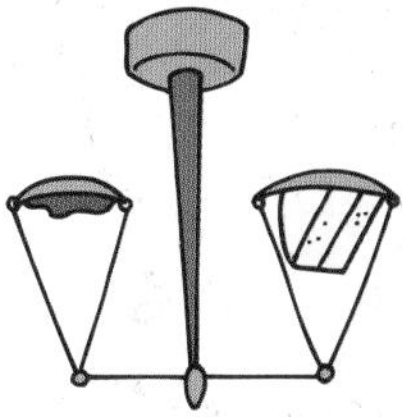

A pound of angel food cake is as heavy as a pound of liver.

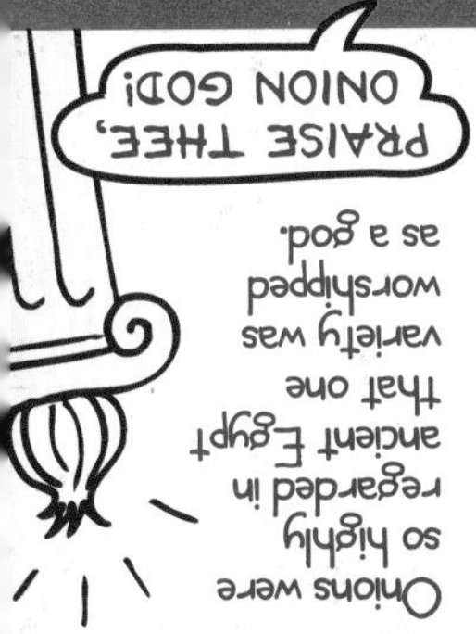

PRAISE THEE, ONION GOD!

Onions were so highly regarded in ancient Egypt that one variety was worshipped as a god.

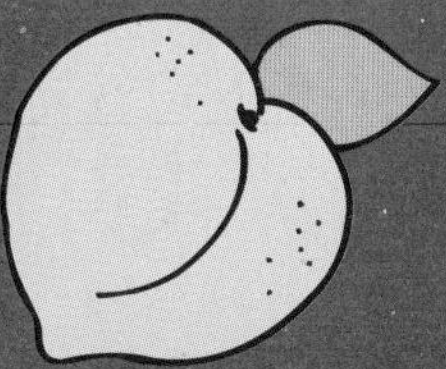

The peach is a Chinese symbol of immortality.

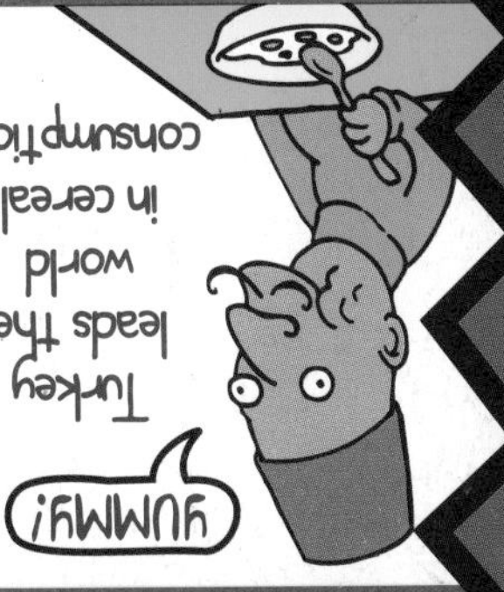

YUMMY!

Turkey leads the world in cereal consumption.

Marrara, a raw meat dish served in southern Sudan, includes urine and bile as flavoring ingredients.

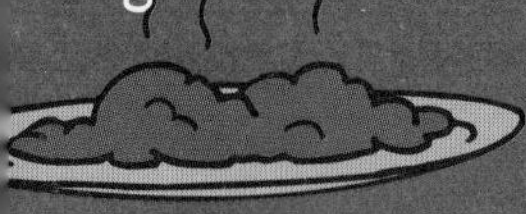

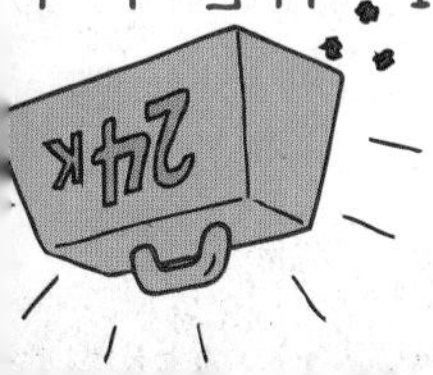

24K

In old England, cloves were wor more than thei weight in gold.

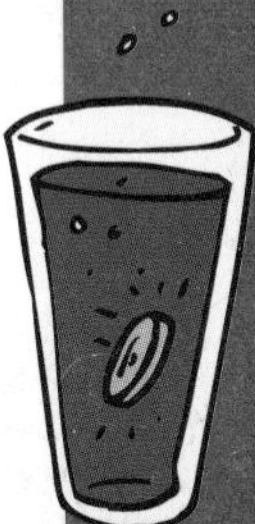

Coke cleans money! Drop a grungy penny into a glass of the stuff and watch it get shiny again!

BOTTOM 12 CEREALS OF ALL TIME

1. OKRA CHEX
2. BARNACLE PETE'S CLAM CLUMPS
3. PUFFED DIRT
4. CREAM O' WIG
5. BEET KRISPIES
6. SHREDDED WOOD
7. GLOOMI-O'S
8. QUAKER HATS
9. KID KUD
10. 7-GRAIN CYRILLIC ALPHABET CHARACTERS
11. LI'L PUFFS O' NUTHIN'
12. SIDESHOW BOB'S BREAKFAST OPTIONS

Yet Even

MORE FO

To eat is human, to stuff divine.
—Marshall Effron

THE WAY-OUT WORLD OF TABLE MANNERS
with your host and tour guide, Bartholomew J. Simpson

In China, one of the most prized dishes is bear's paw soup. (Not as tasty as it sounds!)

In Saudi Arabia, sheep's eyes are a delicacy. (Betcha can't eat just one!)

In Arab countries, never eat with your left hand. (Don't ask us why!)

In the Middle East and the South Pacific, be prepared to eat with your fingers. (Paradise, here I come!)

In Egypt, it is considered impolite to eat everything on your plate. (Which may explain why the Egyptians hate the Bolivians so much.)

In the United States, creamed corn is considered edible. (Believe it or not!)

In Bolivia, you are expected to eat everything on your plate. (Which may explain why the Bolivians hate the Egyptians so much.)

Never eat in any place called "Mom's." —Nelson Algren

A hen is only an egg's way to another egg. —Samuel Butler

A LAND WITH LOTS OF HERRING CAN GET ALONG WITH FEW DOCTORS.
--Prudent Danish proverb

GIVE A DOG AN APPETIZING NAME AND EAT HIM.
--Peculiar Chinese proverb

CABBAGE TWICE COOKED IS DEATH.
--Spooky Greek proverb

SPINACH IS THE BROOM OF THE STOMACH.
--Flamboyant French proverb

OODFUN!

BEWARE!

The following harmless, even appetizing-sounding foods are nothing like what they seem! Don't be fooled by their seductive nicknames!

FOOD NAME	WHAT IT REALLY IS
Tripe	Ox stomach
Sweetbreads	Pancreas or thymus gland of a calf
Variety Meats	Visceral organs
Melt	Spleen
Headcheese	A loaf of jellied and seasoned meats from the head and feet of hogs
Lights	Lungs
Prairie Oysters	Horse or bull testicles

Grub first, then ethics. —Bertolt Brecht

FOOD WITHOUT HOSPITALITY IS MEDICINE.
--Cynical Tamil proverb

IN THIRTY-SIX DISHES ARE SEVENTY-TWO DISEASES.
--Pessimistic Punjabi proverb

HE WHO WOULD HAVE EGGS MUST ENDURE THE CACKLING OF HENS.
--Curious Dutch proverb

GOD SENDS MEAT AND THE DEVIL SENDS COOKS.
--Bitter English proverb

EATING SHOULD BE DONE IN SILENCE, LEST THE WINDPIPE OPEN BEFORE THE GULLET, AND LIFE BE IN DANGER.
--The Talmud

THE DONUT
Nature's Perfect Snack Treat

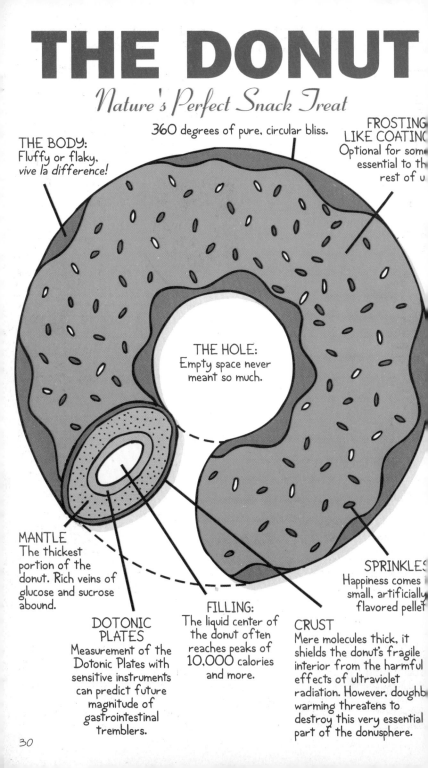

360 degrees of pure, circular bliss.

THE BODY:
Fluffy or flaky, vive la différence!

FROSTING LIKE COATING
Optional for som essential to th rest of u

THE HOLE:
Empty space never meant so much.

MANTLE
The thickest portion of the donut. Rich veins of glucose and sucrose abound.

DOTONIC PLATES
Measurement of the Dotonic Plates with sensitive instruments can predict future magnitude of gastrointestinal tremblers.

FILLING:
The liquid center of the donut often reaches peaks of 10,000 calories and more.

CRUST
Mere molecules thick, it shields the donut's fragile interior from the harmful effects of ultraviolet radiation. However, doughb warming threatens to destroy this very essential part of the donusphere.

SPRINKLES
Happiness comes i small, artificially flavored pellet

30

Homer's **DOZEN-DONUT-A-DAY** Diet

SUNDAY
Doubly Double Chocolatey Chocolate: Worship begins at home.

MONDAY
Plain Cake Lite: Back to work with a healthy attitude.

TUESDAY
Tiny Nuclear Sprinkles: Check the box for fallout!

WEDNESDAY
The Spare Tire: Glazed with Licorice... an acquired taste.

THURSDAY
Pink-Coated: Back to basics.

FRIDAY
T.G.I.F. Thank Goodness It's Five-Flavor-Frosted.

SATURDAY
Powdered Sucrose-Fructose-Dextrose-Glucose: Free at last!

I GO NUTS FOR DONUTS.

WILL YOU BE MY PASTRY PAL?

More About Donuts

Genuine donuts are deep fried exclusively in animal fat. Accept no substitutes.

A chocolate donut contains more calories than a chocolate egg.

Each donut supplies less than 1% of the required daily amount of anything.

Dunking a donut in coffee is considered proper etiquette in most countries.

Somewhere in the world, at any given moment, someone is eating a donut.

The "do" in "donut" is short for "dough."

31

Health & Fitness

The Human Body

Courtesy of Bartholomew Simpson, M.D.

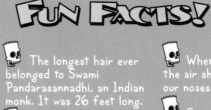

THE HUMAN BODY IS A BEAUTIFUL THING, MAN, BUT BEAUTY'S ONLY SKIN DEEP. BENEATH THE SURFACE LURKS A DISGUSTING AND FRIGHTENING WORLD OF GUTS, GORE AND GLANDULAR DISORDERS. I GIVE YOU LE CORPS HUMAIN, IN ALL ITS GLORY . . .

Still can't wait... ...meaning of life? Turn to page 51...

BONUS BODY FUN FACTS!

💀 The human body contains 3,000,000 sweat glands.

💀 The skin weighs from 6-10 lbs. If it were spread out flat, it would cover an area about 3ft. X 7ft. Normally PMS 116 in color, the skin is the body's largest organ.

💀 The serious, scientific name for the funny bone is the Humerus.

💀 The longest hair ever belonged to Swami Pandarasannadhi, an Indian monk. It was 26 feet long.

💀 The human body is about 2/3 water.

💀 The average person breathes some 13 million cubic feet of air in a lifetime.

💀 Less than half of one kidney can do the work of two kidneys!

💀 When we sneeze, the air shoots out of our noses at 100 mph.

💀 Scientists have recently found that the appendix plays a vital role in the body's well-being and that removal can cause death.

💀 If you get your wisdom teeth pulled you'll become a foolhardy person.

This is what your hair looks like in cross-section if it is:

Straight   Curly   Frizzy   Permed

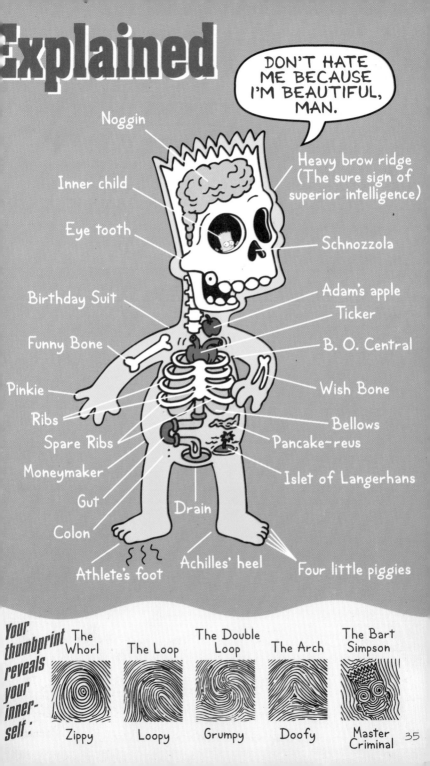

Dr. Bart's Miracle Cures

IF THESE WORK, IT'S A MIRACLE!

HICCUPS

1. Put your elbow in your mouth and hold it there for 30 minutes.

2. Hold your breath, and while you're holding it drink an entire 8 oz. glass of water without stopping to breathe.

3. Turn your pockets inside out.

4. If that doesn't work, turn someone else's pockets inside out.

5. Place a wastebasket on your head and have someone play the drum solo from "In-a-gadda-da-vida."

6. Eat a spoonful of sugar.

7. Have someone run over your toes with a skateboard.

8. Get nose-to-nose with someone you dislike and stare at him or her for 15 minutes.

9. Put ice cubes in your shoes and walk backwards in them for 36 paces.

10. Think of three bald men.

11. Put a bunch of potato bugs in a sack and tie it around your neck with a string.

12. Stand on your head.

13. Accuse the victim of something he or she has not done.

14. Breathe into a paper bag.

15. Bungee jump.

16. Pour salt on your tongue.

17. Bite your thumbs and blow hard against them for one minute.

18. Write "I will not hiccup" 50 times on a blackboard.

19. Whistle in the dark.

20. Eat 10 candy bars. Who cares if the hiccups don't stop?

The real answer to the meaning of life is hidden on page 137...

SUNBURN

Apply an ice-cold Squishee to the affected area. Always remove cup first.

For severe burns, cover your entire body with a salve of blueberry gelatin mixed with avocado paste. Dot with miniature marshmallows.

WARTS

There's an old wives' tale that says frogs give you warts. Not true. Frogs actually can cure warts. To get rid of a wart, spend at least one hour per day fondling, petting, or kissing a frog. After several years, or maybe sooner, the wart should disappear.

HAY FEVER

Apply waffle batter on and around the navel. Leave on overnight. WARNING: If you roll over onto your stomach in the night, it may be difficult to remove yourself from bed in the morning.

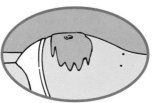

COUGHING

Frogs also make excellent cough suppressants. To get rid of a cough, put a live frog in your mouth, then release it. Repeat 3 times. The cough should disappear, maybe.

Or eat several bowls of chocolate ice cream, followed by a big handful of breath mints. Wash everything down with a bottle of whiskey.

ACNE

Cover pimples with a yellow highlighter.

If condition persists, cover head with a brown paper bag.

ENNUI

a. Avoid any school-related activity for at least a week.

b. Body should be kept in a prone position, preferably in the living room on a long, comfortable sofa.

c. Intensive comic book reading and heavy doses of cartoon watching are advised. These activities have been clinically proven to speed recovery.

LOCKJAW

Unfortunately, there is no cure for lockjaw. However, lockjaw is a great cure for obesity.

IF ALL ELSE FAILS, TAKE TWO ASPIRINS AND CALL ME IN THE MORNING, MAN.

The fine art of BATHING

"Bah, humbug," you say? No way, Jose! Bathing is not only a great way to goof off without getting in trouble, it also keeps the flies away, man.

PREPARATION
You will need:
1. Towel
2. Bath toys
3. A healthy disregard for others

PROCEDURE
1. Turn on water.
2. Once water has filled tub to desired level, hop in.
3. Remove clothing first.

Rule #1: DON'T get your toe stuck in the faucet!!!

The skin of a bubble is only a few millionths of an inch thick.

Heat and dryness are what pop bubbles, not sharpness. You can stick a knife through a bubble and not pop it.

DID YOU KNOW
The Phoenicians in 6th century B.C. were the first people to use soap. They made it by boiling goat fat, water, and ash.

SECRET MYSTERY BATHTIME PLEASURE THEATER 3000
Can you make bubbles in the tub without using your mouth or nose? It's easier than you think!

FOR THE ADVENTUROUS

1. The Human Prune
Sit in the tub for as long as you possibly can (at least an hour). When you get out, your skin will be all wrinkly. Then you can scare the daylights out of your younger siblings by telling them you caught a strange, incurable, highly contagious skin disease in the bathtub.

2. Bathroom Tsunami
Stir up a "storm at sea" by swirling the water in the bathtub around and around your body. Whip things into a frenzy and watch as your toy ships and rubber ducks struggle in vain to stay afloat against the awesome majesty of "Hurricane Jim" or "Typhoon Bob."

3. Voyage to the Bottom of the Tub
Submerge your entire head in the water and see how long you can hold your breath. Or, for you thrill seekers, open your eyes under the water (if it's not too soapy) and take a look around down there, if you dare!

4. The Instant Jacuzzi
Drop several handfuls of seltzer tablets into the water. Luxuriate in your very own bubbling cauldron of delight!

THE BATH VS. THE SHOWER

BATH-
Advantage: The soothing effect of a long, hot soak.

Drawback: The slow realization that you're soaking in your own filth.

SHOWER-
Advantage: You can sing in there and sound pretty damn good.

Drawback: The letdown when you try singing once you're out of there.

The Wild, Wild World of Sudsy Hairdos

The Court Jester

The Mom

The Frisky Billy Goat

Krustina the Clown

The Louis XIV
See how many you can make!

WARNING! Do not bring the following items into the tub with you:
- Snapping turtles
- Instant pancake mix
- Piranhas
- Quick-set cement

39

OOTIES DEMYSTIFIED

THERE ARE MANY MYTHS SURROUNDING THE COOTIE. LET US NOW SORT FACT FROM FICTION.

1. There are no known preventive measures that can be taken against cooties. True. However, a guarded attitude and quick reflexes can help.

2. The cootie has a low intelligence quotient. False. Some scientists have even been able to train cooties to jump through tiny microscopic hoops.

Antennae

Innards

Outers

Tatto

Flagellae

THE COOTIE
(Magnified 10,000,000 X)

MISTLETOE—
Harmless foliage or dangerous decoy?

OH, B'AAART!

THE GOOD NEWS:
Once you hit puberty, you're no longer susceptible to cooties.

THE BAD NEWS:
Once you hit puberty, you are susceptible to acne, among other things.

DANGEROUS COOTIE TRANSMITTERS

HEY, MAN. ADMIT IT. EVEN *YOU* CARE ABOUT YOUR APPE
SO I'VE ENLISTED THE AID OF THE TWO MOST CONVENIEN
PERSONAL GROOMING. (AND CONFIDENTIALLY, *YO*

To remove wrinkles, sleep with a yogurt facial once a week. Make sure to stir up fruit from bottom.

Mix your base with orange food coloring for a more natural look.

Instead of drying your hair with a blow dryer, use a cotton candy machine.

When in doubt about your hair, tease it.

Make sure your outfits suit your type. Just remember the Four Seasonings: Parsley, Sage, Rosemary and Thyme.

The best way to maintain that peaches-and-cream complexion is, of course, mulch of peaches and crea Make sure to remove the fuzz.

Sucking in your stomach n only gives you a slimmer silhouette, it also leaves more room for his.

BY MARGE SIMPSON
the Goddess of
Glamor

Beauty

Gravity is Beauty's Enemy Number One; maintain buoyant thoughts.

Keep your hair looking peppy with static electricity.

Pluck out all your eyebrow hairs.

Never pluck protruding nose hair; death may result. Instead, use a lightweight Weedwacker.

Replace conventional curlers with Ping-Pong balls for a bouncier result.

Always make sure your necklace matches your shoes.

Straighten your eyelashe so that they point straig up, indicating wide-eyed admiration for your belove

To maintain that irresistib "inner glow," visit your nearest nuclear power pla once a week.

Coarseness and vulgarit are unforgivable in a lad that's the man's job.

After a bath, rub toilet water all over your body be sure to flush first.

Always keep your chin ou of the sun.

The number one beauty secret of the Simpsons is winning personality.

Your belt should be buckled at the very last hole, which shows you live life to the fullest.

If you are lucky enough to be bald, polish your head to a brilliant sheen so that the object of your desire may view herself therein.

Get twice the mileage out of your underwear by turning it inside out.
Voilà, fresh as new!

Contact your inner child by grunting and slapping your belly frequently.

Avoid work at all costs. It produces sweat and unsightly calluses.

The way to a man's heart is through his stomach. Show her you've got a lot of heart.

A great way to show your free spirit is by giving an uninhibited manly belch.

Secrets

BY HOMER SIMPSN!
the Swami of
Swank

Do you really want to know the meaning of life? Turn to page 65...

A man's hairstyle should not exceed the height of a croquet ball.

Buttons on clothing are the devil's handiwork — avoid them.

The circle is the most perfect shape in the universe; strive to attain it.

Always wear loafers. That way you don't have to see your shoes to put them on.

Demonstrate your thoughtfulness whenever possible. At the end of the night, a heavy beard can be very helpful in removing your date's makeup.

Flour is an inexpensive substitute for talcum powder. And when sprinkled over your body right after you shower it can keep your clothes in place all day long.

The scent of chili dogs, onions, and beer, when eaten in combination, makes women swoon.

A flower may wow her, but with donuts she'll go nuts.

Always keep your chin out of the rain.

Let it all hang out.

43

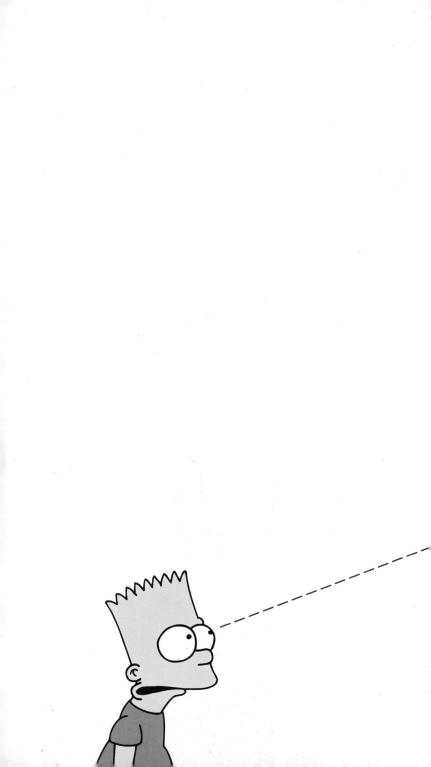

Work & Money

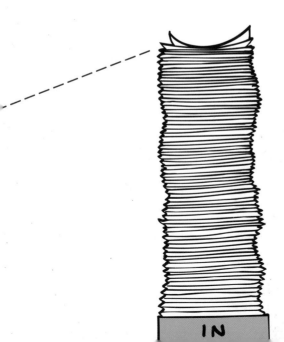

IN

25 COOL THINGS TO BE WhEN YoU GROW UP!

1. Ice Cream Taste Tester

2. Professional Yo-yo-ist

3. Embalmer

4. Millionaire

5. Snake Charmer

6. Vampire

7. Billionaire

8. B-Movie Mogul

9. Monster Truck Racer

10. Water-slide Guinea Pig

11. Tight-rope Walker

25 THINGS NOT TO BE WHEN YOU GROW UP!

1. Street Mime

2. Liposuctionist

3. Wigmaker

4. Galley Slave

5. Political Prisoner

6. Radioactive Waste Collector

7. Envelope Licker

8. Crash Test Dummy

9. Scullery Maid

10. Balloon Animal Artist

11. Romance Novelist

12. Infomercial Host or Hostess

13. Lard Packer

14. Bowling Pin Setter

15. Human Sacrifice

16. Dog Food Cook

21. Leech Farmer

22. Lipstick Tester

17. Septic Tank Repairman

18. Fat Man in a Circus Sideshow

23. Talk-show Host's Wimpy Sidekick

24. Wart Specialist

19. Janitor at an Adult Movie Theater

25. A Clone of Your Parents

20. Republican

49

BART SIMPSON'S E-Z-DOES-IT GUIDE TO

WORK

AND HOW TO AVOID IT AT ALL COSTS

> OUR MOTTO: 99 PERCENT INSPIRATION AND ONLY 1 PERCENT PERSPIRATION, MAN!

WITHOUT EVER GETTING IN TROUBLE!

The true work-avoidance expert is a dogged and dedicated artist. This kind of stuff takes skill, man. So if at first you don't succeed, well, it's probably too much work to really keep trying, so maybe you should just try sneaking off to a movie or something before your parents catch you and make you do more chores.

Then again, if you think you can get it right the first time, you might want to try some of my patented, parent-proof, work-avoidance techniques.

1. Never linger too long after a meal. Those who stay, get stuck putting dishes away. Those who flee, get to watch TV!

2. Always have something more important to do. For example: when asked to clean your room, say you're doing your homework. When told to do your homework, tell 'em you're cleaning your room. Works like a charm!

3. Say "It's ___YOUNGER, WEAKER SIBLING'S NAME HERE___'s turn! I did it last week!" This surprisingly simple trick often works since your parents can't remember much of anything and are depending on you to know the score. WARNING: We don't recommend sticking the chores to older, sneakier, or stronger siblings or you may be sorry.

4. Fake an interest in reading. Just stick your favorite issue of Radioactive Man inside a big, thick, brainy book, bury your nose in it and relax, man. Generally, parents are so excited about your newfound interest they won't bug you for months. If they start to get suspicious, or finally ask you to actually do something, reply in an offended tone, "Can't you see I'm trying to improve my mind?!" Then stomp off to your room in a huff.

> DON'T BUG ME, MAN. I'M ON THE VERGE OF COMPREHENDING THE UNIVERSE.

THE OLD "HOLE IN THE BUCKET" STRATEGY

A Bart Simpson Work-Avoidance Exclusive!

If you must know what the meaning of life is, turn to page 123...

5. Procrastinate to the point where your parent realizes it'll take less time for them to do the task themselves than to show you how to do it. Takes a little patience but the results are well worth it, man.

6. If you're truly desperate to escape the drudgery of home toil, you may want to consider joining an after-school activity. I warn you, though, this can be as grueling as, if not more so than, household chores. You also may be subjected to humiliating rituals and forced to wear ridiculous clothing. Recommended as a last-ditch effort only.

7. Pretend you're hurt or sick. You won't have to lift a finger, and you get the ADDED BONUS FEATURE of being waited on hand and foot by those evil taskmasters themselves—your parents!

BART! SWEEP THE WALKS!

WITH WHAT SHALL I SWEEP THEM?

TRY THE BROOM!

THE BROOM HANDLE'S BROKEN.

THEN FIX IT!

WITH WHAT?

TRY A CURTAIN ROD.

BUT THE CURTAIN ROD'S TOO LONG.

THEN CUT IT!

WHAT WITH?

TRY THE SAW.

WHERE'S THE SAW?

IN THE GARAGE.

THE GARAGE IS TOO MESSY.

THEN CLEAN IT.

WITH WHAT SHALL I CLEAN IT?

USE THE BROOM!

BUT THE BROOM HANDLE'S BROKEN.

REPEAT IF NECCESSARY UNTIL PARENT GETS THE POINT.

51

COOKIES, PAYOLA, DINERO, SMALL POTATOES, WAMPUM, SPINACH, SPONDOOLICKS, BEANS, BISCUIT, FROG SKINS,

FAST CASH

This is the nineties. Selling lemonade just won't cut it anymore, man. A quarter won't buy you squat. Here are some ideas for making mucho dinero, pronto!

THE HARD WAY

$ The Lottery (obviously)

$ Your Mom's Purse
Always a bonanza (especially on Fridays but be careful. If she doesn't get you, your own guilt will.

$ Extortion/Blackmail
Steal your sister's diary, your dad's gambling I.O.U.'s, your brother's skin mags – anything they don't want the rest of the family to see, and charge them big bucks to get them back. Warning: This method may result in your sudden and mysterious disappearance.

THE HARDER WAY

$ Information
We live in the Information Age. Knowledge is power. Keep your eyes and ears open and determine who can benefit most from what you see and hear, and offer it to them for a price. Bookies and stockbrokers do this every day.

TY DOLLAR, DOUGH, BIG BUCKS, PAPER, GREENBACKS, DO RE MI, BREAD,

$ Rewards

Are offered for many things: from
lost cats (check your local phone
poles) to evidence of Bigfoot.
•Project Bigfoot in Seattle,
Washington, will pay $1,000 for
any authentic remains (hair, skull,
teeth or bones) from an actual
Sasquatch. Try to fool 'em with your
Granpa's dentures.

•"America's Most Wanted" will pay
for information leading to the arrest
and conviction of many of America's
most infamous criminals. Also, check
with your local FBI branch and state
banking associations for rewards.
You may be able to collect twice!

•Cutty Sark (in London, England)
will pay $1 million to the person who
captures a spaceship of a being from
outer space. Really. So keep
watching the skies!

LOST CAT
ANSWERS TO "FLAKEY"

REWARD!
OWNERS DESPERATE!!!

THE HARDEST WAY

$ Manual (Ugh!) Labor
As a last resort, many of us are
forced into the most base and mundane
actions. A few standards that stand
the test of time:
•Washing cars (at $5 a car you
could earn $10 an hour which ain't
too shabby.)
•Mowing lawns (the same time and
money factors apply.)
•Sweeping garages (take advantage
of the fact that no homeowner likes
to do this.)

53

55

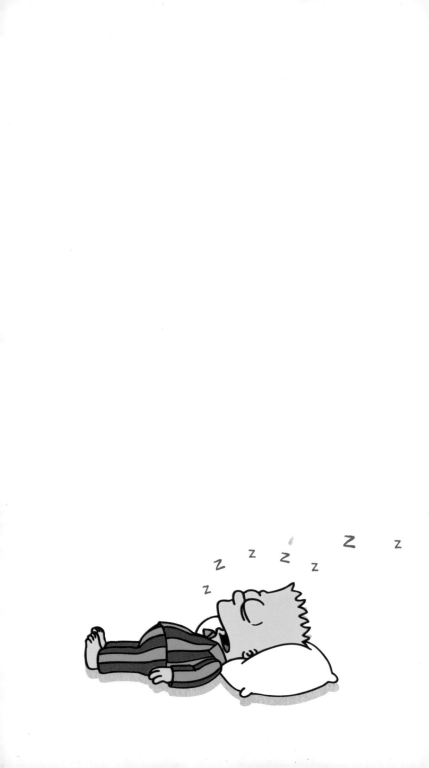

After Hourz

MY DREAM B

① Midnight observatory tower with mega-powered intergalactic telescope
② Personal portrait painted by the most brilliant artist of the 20th century
③ Chart of alien life forms
④ Private basketball court
⑤ Push-button automatic wardrobe selector
⑥ Complete audiovisual home entertainment center featuring Krusty Channel cable hookup
⑦ Model planes' dogfight
⑧ Personal fridge stocked with junk food
⑨ Video Dream Recorder
⑩ Miniature heavy-metal-band alarm clock
⑪ $E=MC^2$ Freeze-Time snooze control
⑫ Breakfast Butler and Midnight Snack Maid robots
⑬ Parent-proof bedroom security door
⑭ Little sister advance detection system
⑮ See-through wall containing giant ant farm
⑯ Thumbprint-identifying entrance locks
⑰ Tattoo machine
⑱ Glow-in-the-dark blanket
⑲ Plastic see-through waterbed with live piranhas
⑳ Tinkle-Matic™ bed-wetting early warning system
㉑ Secret dungeon
㉒ Desk that does your homework for you
㉓ Trap door to tiger cage below
㉔ Security hounds outside 2 1/2-foot-thick lead door
㉕ Complete Radioactive Man comic library with professional celebrity wrestler bedtime readers

My Dream Bedroom

① Glow-in-the-dark map of constellations on the ceiling
② Giant skylight for daytime reading and night-sky viewing
③ Alexander Calder mobile
④ Gothic gargoyles
⑤ Floor-to-ceiling bookshelves with rolling ladder
⑥ Portrait gallery of incredible women throughout history
⑦ Proud white stallion weather vane
⑧ Autographed photo of Bleeding Gums Murphy
⑨ Complete Malibu Stacy doll set, dollhouse, and wardrobes
⑩ Bouquets of fresh flowers from around the world
⑪ Automatic Rapid Eye Movement detector to monitor sleep patterns
⑫ Famous Women Select-a-Dream Series; meet Marie Curie, Sojourner Truth, Sappho, and others while you sleep
⑬ Subliminal nocturnal language learning pillow
⑭ Fluffy sheep to count you to sleep
⑮ A chambermaid
⑯ A classical guitarist for bedtime serenades
⑰ Eiderdown comforter quilted with portraits of famous jazz greats
⑱ Private bedside phone with direct lines to friends and public officials
⑲ Desk made of seashells and fossils
⑳ Subatomic microscope on fully automated science lab-nightstand
㉑ Carpet made of bluegrass

61

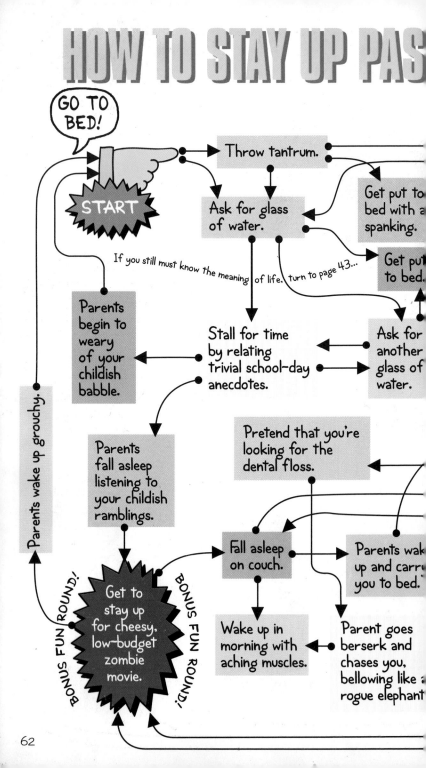

HOW TO STAY UP PAS

If you still must know the meaning of life, turn to page 43...

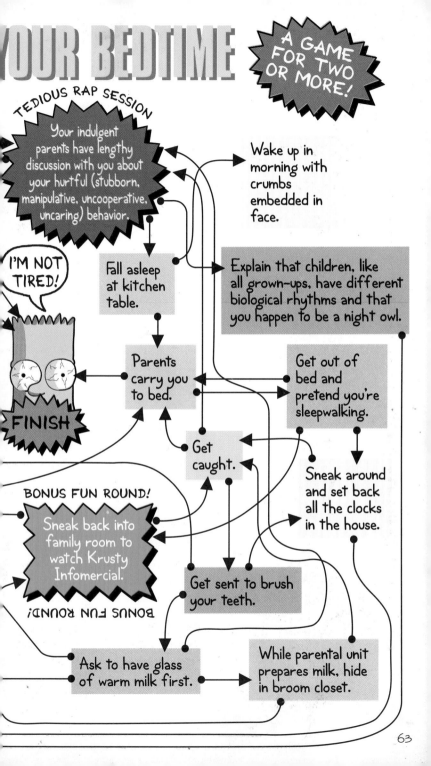

Your Dreams

IF YOU SEE YOURSELF IN A DREAM . . .

IT MEANS . . .

IF YOU SEE YOURSELF IN A DREAM . . .	IT MEANS . . .
naked in a shopping mall	you will become a professional wrestler.
being chased by a giant squid	you will develop a rash.
having your hair cut by dancing policemen	you will get a free backstage concert pass.
with a black eye	you will fall for a practical joke.
floating in a vat of pancake batter	the cards are stacked in your favor.
sitting on thumbtacks	a dog will bite you.
being pulled into the sky by a kite	you will become a movie star.
selling beets to talking pigs	you will be sent to the principal's office.
riding on a black skateboard	you will strike terror into the hearts of your enemies.
skydiving without a chute	someone will tie your shoelaces together.

and what they are trying to tell you:

IF YOU SEE YOURSELF IN A DREAM . . .	IT MEANS . . .
swimming in a lake of Squishees	money will stick to your fingers.
as delicate as a flower	your breath will stink.
gargling creamed corn	you will join the circus.
wrestling a fish	things will slip through your fingers.
dancing with a corndog	you will visit an amusement park.
where it is raining chimneys	you will get a sore throat.
where your parents have become bowling pins	you will be granted a wish.
playing hopscotch on your own stomach	you will lose your lunch.
worshipping rabbits	you will found a media empire.
dreaming you are in a dream	you watch too much TV.

Still pondering the meaning of life? Turn to page 36...

65

Parents

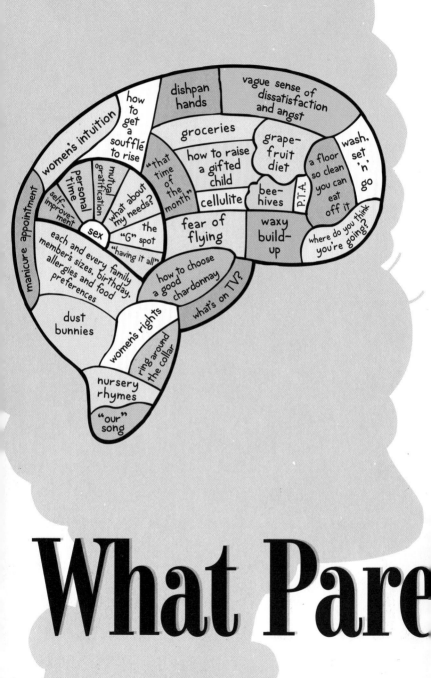

What Pare

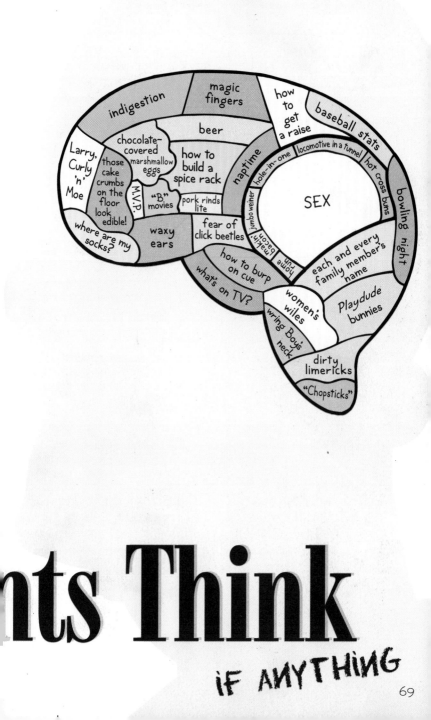

ns Think

IF ANYTHING

69

How to Drive Your Parents Nuts

RULE #1: BE YOURSELF, MAN!

IN THE CAR

2. Forget to go to the bathroom before you leave on a long trip.

3. Ask "Are we there yet?" every 30 seconds.

4. Wait 'til you're on a lonely, barren stretch of highway, then tell them you're really hungry.

5. Whine.

6. Start a contest with your little sister to see who can talk in the squeakiest voice.

7. Offer to drive the car for a while so they can get some shut-eye.

8. Hang BAs at passing policemen.

9. Instigate a rousing round of "99 Bottles of Beer on the Wall."

10. Insist they pick up hitchhikers.

11. Once you've arrived at your destination, say you want to go home.

12. Put your moodiness to work for you with the 4 S's: spitting, sobbing, sulking, and screaming.

13. Instigate a rousing round of "999 Bottles of Beer on the Wall." (For the truly daring!)

ARE WE THERE YET?

SUCK

IN CHURCH

14. Applaud after the sermon.

15. Yell "I have to peepee!"

16. Squirm.

17. Doodle in the missal.

18. During the offering, help yourself to a little change.

19. Fidget.

20. If the minister looks at you, stick out your tongue.

21. Yawn.

22. Burp loudly during the homily.

23. Fall asleep.

24. Stare at the people in the row behind you.

25. Snore.

72

ZIS WAH-TAIR, SHE IZ NOT COLD ENOUGH, GARÇON.

AT FANCY RESTAURANTS

38. Request a booster seat.

39. Call the waiter "garcon."

40. Blow bubbles in your milk.

41. Tie your napkin on your head.

42. Send back your ice water, saying it's not cold enough.

43. Eat everything with your fingers.

44. Ask to see the chef.

45. Ask to have a sip of their wine.

46. Order the most expensive thing on the menu.

47. Eat only a few bites of your meal, then complain of a stomachache.

48. Order dessert.

49. If they refuse to let you have dessert, throw a tantrum.

ALWAYS

50. Tell your parents you love them so much you never, ever want to leave home.

AT THE GROCERY STORE

26. Sneak things into their shopping cart (fake fingernails, corn pads, puffy canned goods, etc.).

27. Claim you're lost and have your mom paged.

28. Practice your juggling with a few grade-A eggs.

29. Lick the fruit.

30. Lie in the freezer case and pretend you're frozen.

31. Rearrange the merchandise.

32. Change the price tags on everything.

33. Eat as much stuff as you possibly can before you get to the checkout line.

34. Demand to sit in the cart.

35. Squeeze the cream filled donuts.

36. Open all the cereal boxes on the shelves and fish out the prizes.

37. See if you can remove the bottom can from the giant canned beet display.

Art & Culture

MUSEUM ETIQUETTE

MUSEUMS ARE OUR HALLOWED HALLS OF CULTURE, BUT DON'T HOLD THAT AGAINST 'EM. THEY DEMAND RESPECT, MAN. SO THE NEXT TIME YOU GET DRAGGED INTO ONE OF THESE DUSTY OLD DUMPS, REMEMBER TO *BEHAVE*. HERE'S HOW:

AT THE NATURAL HISTORY MUSEUM

- Attach bargain price tags to the stuffed animals.
- Tape signs on the backs of museum guards that say "NEANDERTHAL MAN."
- Climb inside a dinosaur skeleton and pretend you're a prisoner of the museum.
- Add your teacher's name to the endangered species list.
- When you look at the wooly mammoth skeleton, ask "Where's the beef?"
- Get into a diorama and pretend you're the hapless victim of a saber-toothed tiger.

HEY!

YOUR HAIRCUT EES COMPLETE, MONSIEUR MONKEY MAN!

INSIGHTFUL QUESTIONS!
(To ask your tour guide)

- "Would you use your gun if that mummy came alive and tried to strangle me?"
- "What's the shelf life of these stuffed warthogs, anyway?"

TOUR GUIDE BRAIN TWISTERS!

- "If an exhibit exploded in another room, and no one was around to hear it, would it make any noise?"
- "Just what is the sound of one hand clapping, anyway?"

AT THE SCIENCE MUSEUM

- Place samples of your saliva on the microscope slides.

- Use the giant magnet to see if any of your classmates have metal plates in their heads.
- Wear a white coat, carry a clipboard, and periodically shout, "Eureka!"
- Ask the tour guide "Do you have any close-up photos of Uranus?"

PARA

HISTORY OF THE UNIVERSE

BANG!

Big Bang

1 Gazillion B.C.
One-celled animals emerge out of primordial ooze.

350 million B.C.

OIN

76

- Ask your tour guide how much longer it will be before a machine takes over his or her job.
- Gently nudge the seismograph and cause major earthquakes.

HANDY PHRASES!

(To Mix 'n' Match)

- "A poignant melding of Rococo and Neo-Classicism."
- "The delicate blend of texture and color radiates sensuality."
- "The juxtaposition of light and shadow creates a curious tension."
- "The artist's inner turmoil reveals itself through the tortured brushstrokes."
- "Ay caramba!"

MoOOOOOO

AT THE ART MUSEUM

- Turn all the modern art paintings upside down and see if anyone can tell the difference.
- Create your own installations using bits of paper, a shoelace, the bread crust from your ham sandwich, and see if the other patrons admire it.
- Examine a blank wall as though there were a painting there.
- Take off all your clothes and pose like a statue. If you get in trouble, reply that the human body is a thing of beauty, as all true artists know, and not something to be be ashamed of.
- Put SOLD stickers on the artwork.
- Tape your teacher's photo to the wall with a note that says "WILL POSE NUDE."

WILL POSE NUDE
SPECIALIZES IN PREEN MAG.S.
FREE
CALL 555-E

AT ANY MUSEUM

- As you go through the museum doors, start mooing like cattle.
- Pretend to touch everything that says "Do not touch." MOOO
- Every museum has an echo. Keep shouting until you find it. MOOO
- Replace the restroom sign with one that says "Special Exhibit This Way."
- Have a contest to see who can slide the farthest on the polished floors. MOO MOOO
- Go fishing for coins in the donation boxes.
- Try to sell your used ticket to some sucker. MoOOOOOO

DO NOT TOUCH

WHOOPS.

To become enlightened about the meaning of life, turn to page 153...

IAC	TRIATHELON	GYMNASTIC	CRETINOUS	FLINTSTONIAN
250 million B.C.	200 million B.C.	150 million B.C.	100 million B.C.	GRRR

TWEET   MEW

DINOSAURS ROAM THE EARTH

HOW TO BE A POETIC GENIUS

Why be a poet? As a full-time job it's the closest thing there is to goofing off. Just being alive is part of your research, man. So you can act any way you want. Whether you're surly and brooding or jumpy and loony, when people find out you're a poet, it explains everything and they leave you alone. Besides, poets get to wear cool hats and play the bongos. Just follow these simple guidelines and study the beautiful poem on the next page and you too can be a poetic genius, man.

1 Dedicate your poem to somebody famous. That way everyone will know you are a deep and important thinker.

2 Always use foreign phrases. It shows you're so smart, one language isn't enough to say what's on your mind.

3 Unfortunately, some poems rhyme. If you have to write one of these, it's easier to pick the words first and find your subject as you go along. Suggestions: eye, why, lie, fly, fie, hi, try, spy, e-coli.

4 The more hopeless the subject of your poem the better. Here are some good topics for starters: hate, love, death, guilt, homework.

5 Punctuation a problem for you? You don't have to use ANY when you write a poem.

6 Or, use ONLY punctuation. Anything goes, man.

7 The bigger the words, the better the poem.

8 Use words that all begin with the same letter. People will be amazed.

9 Here is one of the coolest poetic secrets of all: You don't even need real words. That's right. Just make 'em up.

10 You can write anything you want and call it a poem if you add a lot of space.

11 Spell words any way you want. You are writing the meaning of life, not some dumb rule book.

12 Repeat the same words over and over. Sounds deep, and it fills up the page.

DIG?

THE STONE AGE | THE

2 million B.C.
The dawn of man.

1,250,000 B.C.
Edna Krabappel born.

1,000,000 B.C.
Seymour Skinner born.

400,000 B.C.
Fire invented.

YOWCHIE!

HOW TO BE A Poetic GENIUS*

PART II

HANDY PHRASES FOR THE BUDDING ARTISTIC GENIUS

- When I'm famous, you'll be sorry.

- No one understands me.

- No one understands my work.

- Is there free food at that opening?

- You're all a buncha sellouts.

- Suffering feeds my art.

- Where's my unemployment check?

- Could you front me 10 bucks, man?

- I coulda done that in my sleep.

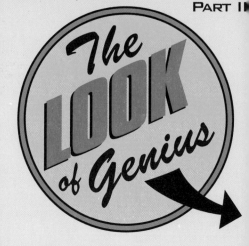

The LOOK of Genius

NOW THAT YOU'VE GOT THE LOWDOWN ON HOW TO WRITE LIKE A GENIUS, IT'S TIME TO LEARN HOW TO PLAY THE PART OF BEING A GENIUS, MAN.

*WORKS JUST AS WELL FOR WOULD-BE PAINTERS, PERFORMANCE ARTISTS, AND MUSICIANS.

THE IRON AGE | THE AGE OF ZINC

2000 B.C. SO MUCH LAUNDRY, SO LITTLE TIME.

800 B.C. Hercules invents body-building.

600 B.C. The Romans invent the circus.

40 B.C. Cleopatra takes baths in tubs of milk.

80

BARTHOLOMEW J. (for JENUINE!) SIMPSON PRESENTS THE

7 WONDERS OF THE WORLD

1. HEIDI, THE SINGING HAMSTER

He doesn't exactly sing, but if you squeeze him just right, his eyes bulge out and he squeaks out the tune to "Big Bad John."

BUY MY "SHROUD OF JEBEDIAH" SAND CANDLES! THEY MAKE GREAT GIFTS!

2. THE SHROUD OF JEBEDIAH SPRINGFIELD

An eerie impression somewhat resembling the head of Springfield's town founder stares back at the viewer from this old dishrag. To witness the amazing spectacle, the faithful line up outside Moe's Tavern, where the shroud was first discovered over four years ago. Some say the image is nothing more than a gravy stain, but to the faithful it is truly a miracle.

3. JASPER'S DENTURES

No one knows how it is that these incredible teeth actually receive radio transmissions from 12 FM stations, 22 AM stations and the police channel, but they do! Scientists have been probing into the phenomenon, trying to explain how this mysterious "receiver" works, but so far have come up empty-handed.

The answer to the true meaning of life awaits you on page 77...

TRULY AMAZING!

THE DARK AGES   THE M

1193
Robin Hood fights the Sheriff of Nottingham.

1194
Friar Tuck founds the first fast-food chicken franchise.

4. MY AUNT PATTY'S BRA

We won't venture to guess at the actual size, but suffice it to say that each cup holds over thirteen pints of milk!

NOT ACTUAL SIZE!

THIS SIGN WAS ONCE 38 FEET TALL!

WARNING! DON'T STAND TOO LONG IN ONE SPOT!

5. THE DEVIL'S SINKHOLE

Countless daredevils have attempted to trudge across this swampy, foul-smelling fen, but none have made it without the loss of at least one shoe. What unearthly phenomenon could have created this all-consuming bog, we may never know. Formerly the site of The Devil's Corroded Cesspool.

6. MARGE SIMPSON'S HAIRDO

Made up of over 170,000 hairs and held together with only a single bobby pin, this Mt. Everest of hairstyles looms above all other bouffants in Springfield . . . and beyond! What secret wonders does it conceal within? We may never know, but it once housed a nest of starlings in its upper regions.

36 ACRES OF FUN, SURROUNDED BY AN ELECTRIC FENCE!

7. KRUSTYLAND AMUSEMENT PARK

Undoubtedly the greatest of the Seven Wonders, at least in our opinion. Thrill-tastic rides include: The Remarkable Leaky Tugboat, Cactus Patch, and the Never-ending Line! Not responsible for vomiting, loss of limbs, drowning, impalement, or heat exhaustion. Sorry, no refunds.

EXPERIENCE THE HINDENBURG! OUR NEWEST SHRIEK-TACULAR RIDE!

DIUM AGES | **THE LIGHT AGES**

1200
Atlantis sinks.

1259
The English cut off an enemy head and kick it around the streets, inventing soccer.

1300
The Black Death wipes out most of Europe.

JULIET

1444
Romeo and Juliet fall in love and die.

Science

BART'S LAWS

We hold these truths to be self-evident.
Do not try to avoid these laws,
for they refuse to be avoided.

*Body
at rest*

*Parental
body*

BART'S FIRST LAW OF MOTION:
A body at rest remains at rest until a parental bod
comes over and tells it to mow the lawn. If that
body continues to remain at rest despite
the urgings of the parental
body, see Bart's Second
Law of Motion.

Velo

BART'S UNIVERSAL LAW OF MOTION:
What goes up
must come down,
man.

Force

T H E   A G E   O F   P O R K

T H E   A G E   O

1471
Count
Dracula
born.
86

1492
Columbus
gets lost and
discovers
America.

1559 Montezuma's
Ice cream   Revenge
invented.

WHO'S LAUGHING NOW?

1586
Francis Bac
invents the
breakfast t
named for

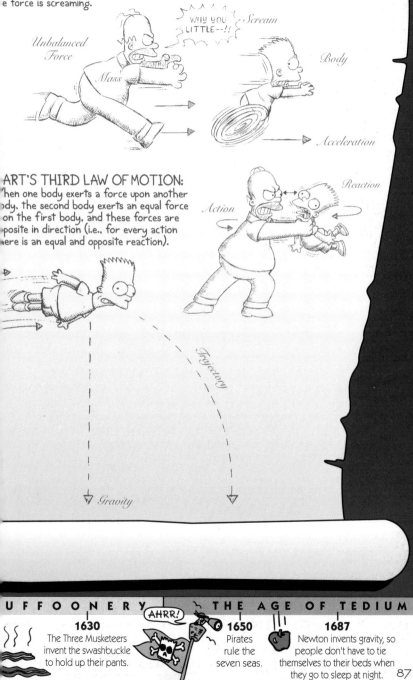

ART'S SECOND LAW OF MOTION:

he acceleration produced by an unbalanced force acting on a body is directly proportional
 the mass of the force plus whether or not the force is carrying a weapon plus how loud
e force is screaming.

Unbalanced Force

Mass

WHY YOU LITTLE--!!

Scream

Body

Acceleration

ART'S THIRD LAW OF MOTION:

'hen one body exerts a force upon another
dy, the second body exerts an equal force
on the first body, and these forces are
posite in direction (i.e., for every action
ere is an equal and opposite reaction).

Action

Reaction

Trajectory

Gravity

U F F O O N E R Y   T H E   A G E   O F   T E D I U M

AHRR!

1630
The Three Musketeers
invent the swashbuckle
to hold up their pants.

1650
Pirates
rule the
seven seas.

1687
Newton invents gravity, so
people don't have to tie
themselves to their beds when
they go to sleep at night.   87

a lurch of drunkards
a frenzy of psychopaths
a snide of gossips
a drab of accountants
a flatter of hairdressers
a slither of yes-men
a tremble of freshmen
a scrimp of landlords
a shallow of debutantes
a sloth of roommates
an annoyance of mimes

a carp of critics
a gripe of actors
a bombast of politicians
a dribble of Republicans
a stubble of uncles
a bleak of pessimists
a slack of procrastinators
a drone of teachers
a groan of comedians

an ooze of network executives
a squelch of chaperones
a swaddle of baby-sitters
a grumpy of principals
a deft of magicians
a chill of assassins
a scam of televangelists
a creep of thieves
a muddle of experts

a bawl of infants
a pester of perfectionists
a squint of astronomers
a cram of students
a shout of ventriloquists
a quagmire of bureaucrats
a drub of bullies
a primp of fashion models
a crimp of chiropractors
a cruller of dieticians
a briny of sailors
a chirp of cheerleaders
a gloat of millionaires
a prey of lawyers

THE AGE OF TOMFOOLERY

1760
Wigs grow to six feet in height in France.

1789
Lots of French people get their heads cut off.

SACRÉ BLEU!

1800
Davy Crockett invents the coon-skin cap.

WELL I'LL BE DANGED!

89

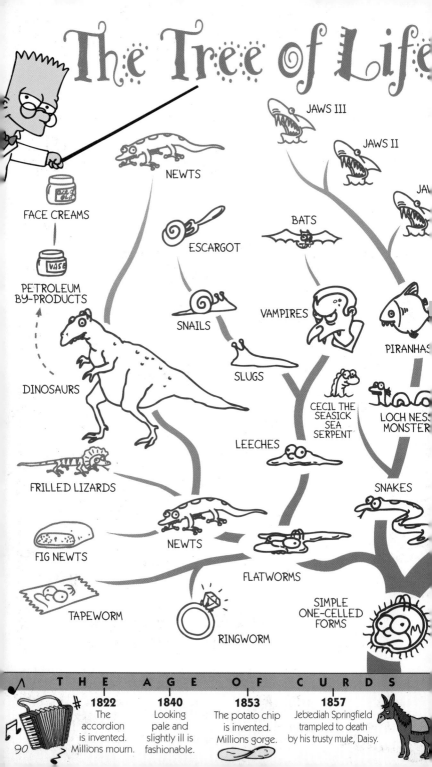

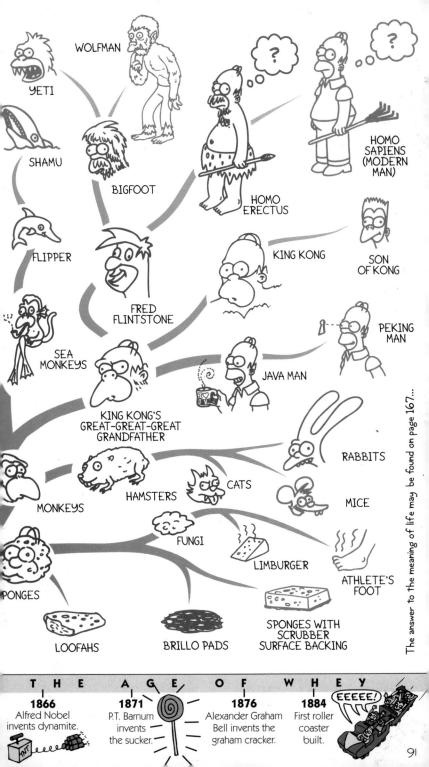

YETI

WOLFMAN

?

?

HOMO SAPIENS (MODERN MAN)

SHAMU

BIGFOOT

HOMO ERECTUS

FLIPPER

KING KONG

SON OF KONG

FRED FLINTSTONE

PEKING MAN

SEA MONKEYS

JAVA MAN

KING KONG'S GREAT-GREAT-GREAT GRANDFATHER

RABBITS

HAMSTERS

CATS

MICE

MONKEYS

FUNGI

LIMBURGER

ATHLETE'S FOOT

PONGES

SPONGES WITH SCRUBBER SURFACE BACKING

LOOFAHS

BRILLO PADS

The answer to the meaning of life may be found on page 167...

T H E   A G E   O F   W H E Y

1866
Alfred Nobel invents dynamite.

1871
P.T. Barnum invents the sucker.

1876
Alexander Graham Bell invents the graham cracker.

1884
First roller coaster built.

EEEEE!

LOW-COST MEDICINE!

Grow a penicillin culture on an ordinary piece of bread.

SAVE THE WORLD!

Light travels at 186,000 miles per second in a vacuum.

THE AMAZING ANTI-GRAVITY BO

Balance a spoon on your nose!

secret tip
use glue.

Light from the sun takes 8.3 minutes to reach the earth.

LAST-MINUTE SCIENCE EXPERIMENTS

If you weigh 150 lbs on earth on Sirius B you would weigh 38,000 tons and would be instantly squashed into a slippery puddle of slimey goop

THE REMARKABLE EXPLODING POP CAN!

1) Shake well.

2) Open.

KRU COL

EXTRA-CREDIT FUN PROJECT
See if you can spray it all over the teacher's pet!

A BRIEF HISTORY OF DROOL

What makes dogs salivate more?

1) A juicy steak?

or

2) A piece of kale?

THE AGE OF FRIVOLITY

1888
Jack the Ripper terrorizes London.

1889
Vincent van Gogh cuts off his ear. Bleeds profusely.

1900
Freud invents dreams; formerly known as indigestion.

First person known to spontaneously combust.

1905
E=mc2

92

THE MIND-BOGGLING LOOP of ETERNITY

1. Cut a strip of paper 1/2" wide by 18" long.

2. Twist once, then tape or glue ends together, forming a "figure 8."

3. Cut the loop in half, lengthwise.

What do you get? 2 loops? Not if you did it right, man!

Fun! The TINGLER

Rub your feet back and forth on a carpet (works best on dry days!) then surprise an unsuspecting subject.

DISCOVER THE AMAZING WORLD OF STATIC ELECTRICITY!

Take bets on what'll happen when you cut it and get rich!

THE ASTOUNDING PAPER AIRPLANE

Demonstrate the fascinating properties of aerodynamics! (This is one paper airplane you can't get sent to to the principal's office for!)

Galileo's Delight

Drop a water balloon and a balloon filled with maple syrup out of the 3rd story window and onto the 5th grade bullies* below.

1. Which balloon lands first?

2. Which bully looks the most unhappy?

3. How many shampooings do you think it will take before they get all that maple syrup out of their hair?

WARNING: Don't let 'em see 'ou or 'ou're 'ead 'eat!

The Ticking Time Bomb

Discover precisely how long it takes to push your teacher over the edge and straight into early retirement.

KEEP THAT SPIKY HAIRED LITTLE DEMON AWAY FROM ME!

HE AGE OF CHURLISHNESS | ROARING TWENTIES

1906 The hot dog created.

1912 Titanic sinks.

POO!

1922 Whoopee cushion invented.

1925 Television invented. Millions stare.

1926 Houdini gets punched in stomach and dies. 93

Language & Communication

REAL LANGUAGES YOU COULD LEARN

Nupe
Urdu
Zande
Dimli
Tho
Rundi
Swahili
Karen
Futa Jalon
Zulu
Dogri
Edo
Tongan
Min
Sango
Kongo
Kamba
Dong
Fon
Tulu
Nung
Somali
Lubu
Makua
Ho
Gogo
Fula
Tatar
Wu
Yao
Yi
Fang-bulu
Chiga
Thonga
Riff
Luba-lulua
Haya
Gondi
Oromo
Pedi
Punjabi
Twi-fante
Uzbek
Wolof
English

To the thieving dog who didn't pay for this book: Your days are numbered, man.

SECRET SHHH!

The Classic **PIG LATIN**

Take the first letter off each word and move it to the back of the word and add an "ay." If the word starts with a vowel (antsy, oink, egghead) just add "ay" at the end of it (antsy-ay, oink-ay, egghead-ay).

WHAT'S THE POINT OF HAVING A SECRET LANGUAGE? SO PEOPLE CAN'T QUARGLE[1] WHA YOU'RE BORFING, FIRKY[3]! SO CHUMBO[4] THESE ZIPLICKS[5] CAREFUL AND SOON YOU'LL BE FLOOMING[6] WITH THE BEST OF 'EM, PIPLA.[7]

ET'S-LAY ISS-KAY ART-BAY!

O-NAY AY-WAY, AN-MAY!

THE AGE OF GANGSTERS

Ignazio "Morning Breath" Vincenza   Vince "Bubble Butt" Carerra   Jimmy "The Hump"   Frank "Bad Dandruff" Luciano   Joey "Unpleasant Armpit Odor" Peretti   Gordy "Four Hairs" Correlli

96

LANGUAGES

OPPISH

An alternative to Pig Latin for the true aficionado.

Rule: Insert "op" after the first consonant of any syllable. For example: "Dude" becomes "dop-ude," "groovy" becomes "grop-oo-vop-y," and "skateboard" becomes "skop-ate-bop-oard."

And now a complete sentence! Normal worn-out English: Don't you dare sass me, young man!

Oppish: Dop-on't yop-ou dop-are sop-ass mop-ee, yop-oung mop-an!

When a word begins with a vowel (odd, ignoramus, elbow) you start the word with "op" (op-odd, op-ig-nop-o-rop-a-mop-us, op-el-bop-ow).

Hold this page up to a mirror and turn it upside down to read the secret message in the panel.

ALPHABET UPSIDE-DOWN-BACKWARDS-CRAZY.

Be the Leonardo da Vinci of your basil! He liked secret languages too, so he wrote down and everything upside backwards in order to keep people from stealing his ingenious ideas. This was explains This his helicopter why his plans never stink got off the ground.

If you don't know the secret message in the panel... He aged to guining of it by now, turn

LET'S GROOPLE,[8] YOU BIG CRENOOTIE[9]

1. UNDERSTAND
2. SAYING
3. STUPID
4. STUDY
5. PAGES
6. COMMUNICATING SECRETLY
7. MAN
8. SNUGGLE
9. HUNK O' MAN

THE INDUSTRIAL AGE | THE ATOMIC AGE

1930 First Twinkie baked. Pastry making reaches its zenith.

1937 Hindenburg explodes.

1945 First atomic blast.

1945 Slinky introduced.

1945 Tangled Slinkys drive millions insane.

SOMETIMES ~~SPEAK LOUDER THAN~~
ACTIONS WORDS

YOUR HANDY GUIDE TO GESTURES 'ROUND THE GLOBE

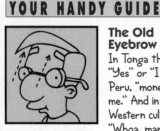

The Old Eyebrow Raise
In Tonga this means "Yes" or "I agree." In Peru, "money" or "Pay me." And in most Western cultures, "Whoa, mama."

The Fingertip Kiss
Common throughout Europe and most Latin American countries. Signifies "Ahh, beautiful!" or "Marveloso!"

The Ear Grasp
Grabbing one's ears in India is a sign of repentance or sincerity. In Brazil, a similar gesture signifies appreciation.

The Head Tap
In Argentina and Pe this means "I'm thinking" or "Think. In other places, it ca mean "He/She is crazy."

The Nose Thumb
A sign of mockery in most European countries. A more emphatic variation is the double-handed nose thumb.

The Protruding Tongue
In many Western cultures, sticking out the tongue signifies contempt or defiance toward the object of the gesture.

The Head Nod
In most countries, this gesture means "Yes." However, in Bulgaria and Greece it means "No."

Blinking the Eyes
In Taiwan, it is considered an impolite gesture to blink your eyes at someone.

THE GOLDEN AGE OF SCI-FI MONSTER MOVIES

1951
Spitzilla

1952
Radio Active Man becomes radioactive.

1953
Hamstron–the Hamster from Beyond Infinity

1957
Creature from the Bottom of the Septic Tank

1958
The Brain Gobblers

BEATNIKS ROAM THE EARTH

T U V W X y Z

The Horizontal Horns
Throughout most European countries, this gesture is used as protection against evil spirits.

The Hand Saw
In Colombia, when you make a deal to share profits, you hold one hand palm down and make a sawing motion across it with the other hand.

The Vertical Horns
In Brazil and other Latin American areas, a sign of good luck. In Italy, though, this means you're being cuckolded.

The Left-Handed Taboo
In many cultures, it is considered rude to offer anything with the left hand, since that hand is used for cleansing oneself.

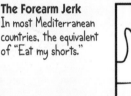

The Forearm Jerk
In most Mediterranean countries, the equivalent of "Eat my shorts."

The Palm Push
In Nigeria, pushing the palm forward with the fingers spread is a vulgar gesture.

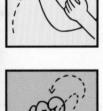

The "Come Hither"
In most Middle Eastern and Far Eastern countries, it's an insult to use the fingers to call someone over to you.

The Finger Circle
In the U.S. we know this t' mean "Okay," but in Brazi' it's considered obscene. In Greece it's impolite, in Japa' it means "money" and in southern France, "zero" or "worthless."

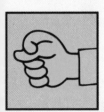

The "Fig"
An obscene gesturc of contempt in some Mediterranean and European lands. In Brazil and Venezuela, though, it's a good luck symbol.

Folded Arms
In Fiji, this is a sign of disrespect. In Finland, a sign of arrogance and pride.

TRANSITIONAL PERIOD   THE AGE OF AQUARIUS

1958
First skateboard sold.

1960
Sea Monkeys debut.

1963
Krusty the Clown gets his start in show biz, appearing on the show *Pulver Lawn Products Presents the Clowns of Tomorrow.*

1969
First man on moon brainwashed by aliens. 99

HOW TO BE A TRANSCO[

Original Bartism	Foreign Language	Written Translation
NO WAY, MAN.	ITALIAN	Má vattene.
	CHINESE	没门，伙计．
	PORTUGUESE	Nem morta, filha.
	RUSSIAN	**ЛАЖА, ЧУВАК**
	FRENCH	Pas question, mon vieux.
	JAPANESE	いや な こった よ．
	GERMAN	Nix da, Alter.
	SPANISH	Ni loco, tio.
EAT MY SHORTS.	ITALIAN	Manco per le palle.
	CHINESE	滚 蛋．
	PORTUGUESE	Eu não tô nem aí.
	RUSSIAN	**НА-КА ВЫКУСИ**
	FRENCH	Lâche moi la grappe.
	JAPANESE	おい なめん な よ．
	GERMAN	Du kannst mich mal im Mondschein begrüssen.
	SPANISH	Chupame el culo.
DON'T HAVE A COW, MAN.	ITALIAN	Non t'incazzare ragazzo.
	CHINESE	冷静 一点 ．
	PORTUGUESE	Fica frio, cara.
	RUSSIAN	**НЕ ПСИХУЙИ, ЧУВАК**
	FRENCH	T'excite pas, mec.
	JAPANESE	あんた ピリピリ する こと ない じゃん．
	GERMAN	Reg Dich ab, Mann.
	SPANISH	No te calientes, hermano.

T H E   E R A   O F   S H A M E

Streaking fashionable.

100

1973 Astronomers see rings around Uranus.

1974 Homer Simpson actually manages to graduate from high school due to a clerical error.

Richard Nixon resigns in shame.

Phonetic Translation	English Approximation
mah VAH-teh-nay.	But get out of here.
MAY muhn HOO-OH-gee.	No door.
NAYN MOHRR-tah FEEL-yah.	Not even dead, daughter.
LAH-zha choo-VAK.	Puddle, dude.
pah keh-steeOHN, mohn vee-UH.	No question, old one.
ee-YAH nah KOH-tah yoh.	An unpleasant thing!
neeks dah AHL-tah.	Nothing there, old one.
nee LOH-koh, TEE-oh.	Not even crazy, uncle.
MAHN-ko pare lay PAH-lay.	Not even for my testicles.
GWEN DAN	Roll egg.
IEoh nah-oh TOH NAYN IE-ee.	I am not even there.
nah-kah VOO-ee-koo-see.	Bite through.
lash mwah la GRAHP.	Let go of my grape.
OY nah-MEN nah yoh.	Hey, don't lick me!
doo kanst meekh mahl im MOHN-shighn bee-GROO-sin.	You can greet me sometimes in the moonshine.
choo-PAH-may el COO-loh.	Lick my butt.
nohn TEEN-kah-TSAH-ray rah-GAHT-soh.	Don't get pissed off, kid.
LUNG CHING EE-dee-ehn.	Cold and quiet, a little.
FEE-kah FREE-oo, KAH-rah.	Stay cold, dude.
nyeh puh-see-HOO-ee, choo-VAK.	Don't psycho, man.
teck-SEET pah, mehk.	Don't get excited, man.
AHN-tah PEE-ree-PEE-ree SOO-roo KOH-toh NAH-ee ZHAHN.	You'd better not be "electric."
rayg deekh AHP, mahn.	Excite yourself down, man.
noh tay cah-lee-EN-tess, ayr-MAH-noh.	Don't overheat, man.

T H E   P O L Y E S T E R   A G E

Gerald Ford falls down.

1975 Platform shoes fashionable.

The leisure suit makes dressing hassle-free.

ARF!

Pet rocks and mood rings cover the Earth.

1976 "Pong" heralds the birth of the video game.

HOW TO BE A TRANSCO...

Original Bartism	Foreign Language	Written Translation
AY CARAMBA!	ITALIAN	Mannaggia la miseria!
	CHINESE	见鬼!
	PORTUGUESE	Ai caramba!
	RUSSIAN	**ТВОЮ МАТЬ** !
	FRENCH	Ay caramba!
	JAPANESE	アレ マア!
	GERMAN	Sack Zement!
	SPANISH	Carajo!
I HAVE AN ANNOUNCEMENT TO MAKE: I'M BORED.	ITALIAN	Devo fare un importante annuncio: Sono scazzato.
	CHINESE	我要宣布一个通告. 我感到很无趣.
	PORTUGUESE	Eu tenho um anunciamento à fazer: Eu tô de saco cheio
	RUSSIAN	**УСТАЛ Я СЛУШАТЬ**
	FRENCH	J'ai une déclaration à faire: Je me fais chier.
	JAPANESE	みんな ちょっと ちょっと. つまう ん
	GERMAN	Ich hab ne Ankündigung zu machen: Mir ist langweilig.
	SPANISH	Tengo un anuncio: Estoy podrido.
OUTTA MY WAY, MAN.	ITALIAN	Levati dalle palle.
	CHINESE	滚开.
	PORTUGUESE	Sai da frente, cara.
	RUSSIAN	**ОТВАЛИ**
	FRENCH	Dégage, mec!
	JAPANESE	あっち へ 行き な.
	GERMAN	Hau ab.
	SPANISH	Salite del medio, loco!

T H E   M E   D E C A D E   N E

1980 Greediness becomes a religion. Millions worship.

1982 Wacky Wallwalker fad.

Fezzes are haute couture.

1989 Being openly greedy goes out of vogue.

1990 The Bart Simpson decade begins.

1991 The cupcak perfected by Marge Simpson.

102

Phonetic Translation	English Approximation
mah-NAHJ-jah lah MEE-sayr-EE-ah!	Damn to the misery!
CHEE-EHN GWAY!	Meet ghost!
Iee cah-RAHM-bah!	Ay caramba!
tuh-VOY-oo MAHT!	Your mama!
I cah-ROOM-bah!	Ay caramba!
AH-ray MAAAH!	Serious!
sahk tseh-MENT!	Sack of cement!
gah-RAH-ho!	Yikes!
DAY-voh FAH-ray oon im-por-TAHN-tay ah-NOON-seeoh: SOH-noh skah-TSAH-toh.	I have an announcement to make: I'm bored.
WOHR YOW SHOO-en-poo EE-guh TOHN-gow: WOHR GAHN tow hung WOO lee-ow.	I have an announcement to make: No fun.
AYoh TAYN-yoh oom ah-NOON-see-yah-MAYN-toh ah FAH-ZAYRH: AYoh toh deh SAH-coh SHAY-oo.	I have an announcement to make: My bag is full.
oo-STAHL yah SLOO-shihUHT.	Tired I listening.
jay oon deh-klah-ra-seeOHN ah FAYR: juhm fay sheeAY.	I have a declaration to make: I make myself dump.
mee-NAH CHOH-toh CHOH-toh. tsoo-mah-RAH nn	Everybody, a little, a little. A trifle.
eekh hahb nuh AHN-kuhn-dee-goong tsoo MAHK-en: meer ist LAHNG-vie-lig.	I have an announcement to make: I'm bored.
TENG-oh oon ah-NOON-see-oh: es-TOY poh-DREE-doh.	I have an announcement to make: I'm rotting.
lay-VAH-tee DAH-lay PAH-lay.	Go off my testicles.
GWEN KIGH.	Roll away.
SIGH-ee dah FREN-chee, KAH-rah.	Get out of my front, dude.
uht-vah-LEE.	Roll away.
day-GAHJ, mehk.	Get lost, man!
ah-CHEE-ay EE-KEE-NAH.	Go away.
how AHP.	Get lost.
sah-LEE-tay del MAY-dee-oh, LOH-coh!	Get out of the middle, crazy person!

A G E | **N E W** **A G E** **L I T E**

1992
Infomercials surpass network programming in entertainment value.

1993
Looking pale and slightly ill is fashionable.

1993
Homer forgets Marge's birthday again, maintaining a perfect record.

Platform shoes fashionable.

The Livin' End

Animals

THE 9 TYPES OF DOGGIES

THE TINKLER

(also known as Pee Dog, Stain Master 2000, and The Wiz)
PROS:
Always happy to see you.
CONS: Pees when happy.

DROOLY

(also known as Throat Gravy, Sir Saliva-lot, and Rabid)
PROS: Can survive for weeks off his own bodily fluids.
CONS: Flicks his spittle on everything, including you.

OL' SMELLER

(also known as Stinky, Silent-But-Deadly, and Odor-Licious)
PROS: Stays put.
CONS: His smell follows you everywhere.

LAZY-BOY

(also known as The Lump, Lord Snoozington, No-Good-Sack-O-Bones)
PROS: Requires very little attention.
CONS: Could be dead for weeks before you realize it.

LI'L SHAKEY

(also known as Tremble-ina, Flinchy, and Mr. Quivers)
PROS: Will always do as she's told.
CONS: Flinches when spoken to.

BRUTUS MAXIMUS

(also known as Snappy, Chompy,
and Nice Doggie)
PROS: Can rip your enemies to shreds.
CONS: May confuse you with your enemies.

THE YAPPER

(also known as The Yipper,
The Yopper, and Shut Up)
PROS: Good watchdog.
CONS: May not live long.

THE PSYCHO

(also known as
Little In-Bred,
Snake-in-the-Grass,
and Take-Yer-Chances)
PROS: Pleased to meet you.
CONS: Pleased to eat you.

WONDER-PUP

(also known as Love of My Life,
Man's Best Friend, and Sweetie)
PROS: Dog o' your dreams.
CONS: Could change at any minute into
one of the 8 other types of doggies.

DOG YEARS

Every year of our lives
is equal to about
7 dog years.
Here are some
comparative
time scales.

Distance from
earth to the nearest
star (4 light-years)
= 28 dog light-years

Time it takes on
average to bathe
your dog (26
minutes) = 3 hours
and 2 minutes
in dog years

Length of time it
takes to get through
school (12 years) =
84 dog years

Durration of a dog
day afternoon
(6 hours) =
42 dog hours

Age of the universe
(60,000,000,000 years)
= 420,000,000,000
dog years

Overwhelming desire to please

LET'S PLAY!

Large, extra-sensitive ears that can hear a pin drop 250 miles away, or your sister whispering on the telephone in the next room

Mythical appendage

Brain large enough to understand everything you say

A nose that can balance beach balls and catch Frisbees

Friendly disposition

Breath that smells like peppermint

Breathes fire

Long, giraffelike neck for peeking over trees and around corners

Long, silky coat

Suction cups on feet for walking on ceilings

Webbed toes for fast swimming

The Ultimate Dream Pet

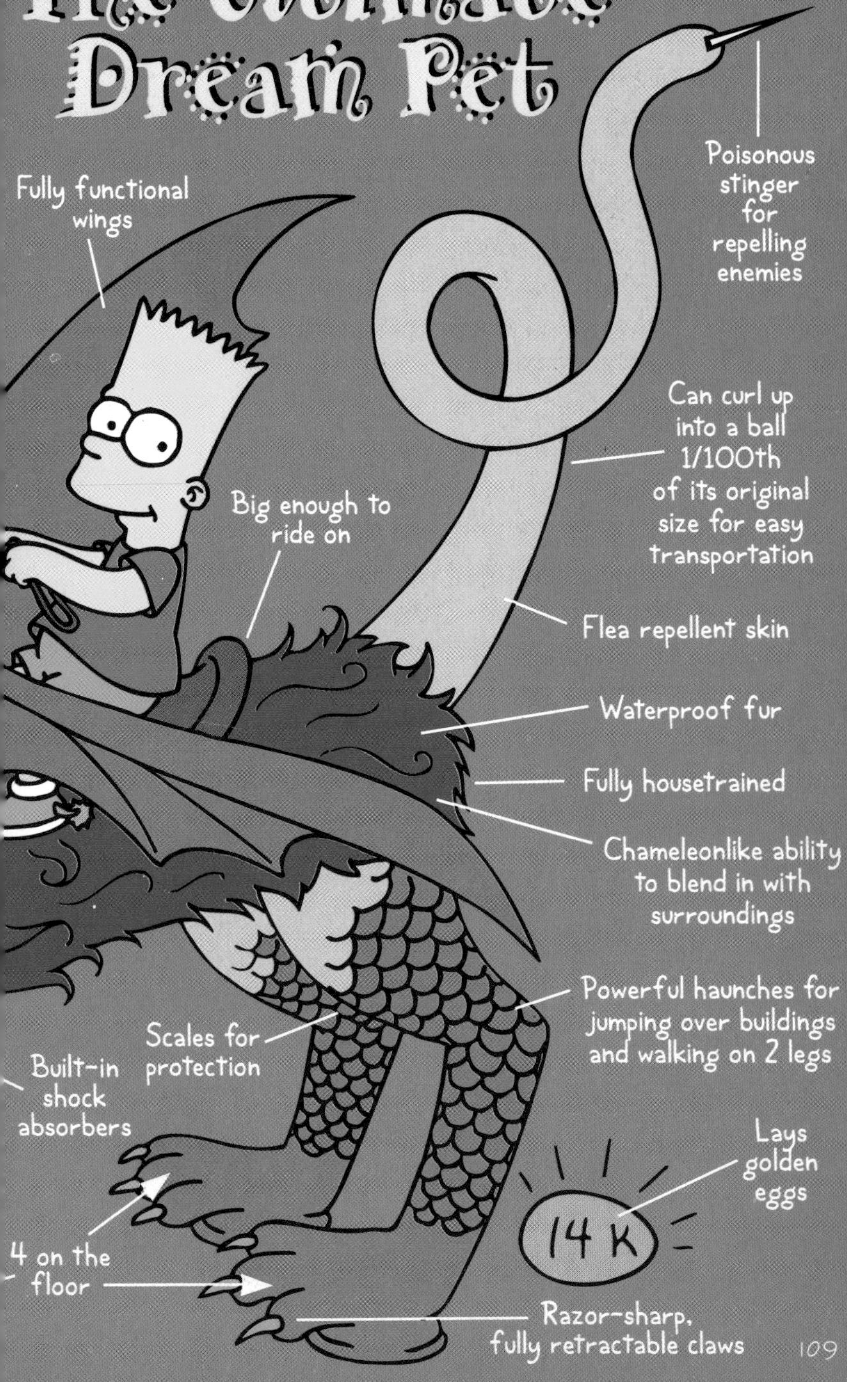

Fully functional wings

Poisonous stinger for repelling enemies

Big enough to ride on

Can curl up into a ball 1/100th of its original size for easy transportation

Flea repellent skin

Waterproof fur

Fully housetrained

Chameleonlike ability to blend in with surroundings

Powerful haunches for jumping over buildings and walking on 2 legs

Scales for protection

Built-in shock absorbers

Lays golden eggs

14 K

4 on the floor

Razor-sharp, fully retractable claws

ANIMAL GROUP NAMES

ANIMAL BRA

Your average, everyday, run of the mill mosquito has 47 teeth.

THE SILKWORM
is neither silk,
nor is it a
worm. It is a
caterpillar.

THE HAMSTER
is neither a ham, nor
do you stir it. It is a
furry rodent, related
to the guinea pig.

A bee has to beat her wings 720 times a second to stay in the air.

THE JACKALOPE
is neither named
Jack, nor does it
lope. It is a bunny
with antlers.

Bedbugs bark enthusiastically whenever they smell human fles

THE HEDGEHOG is neither
a hedge, nor is it a hog.
It is a small, insect-eating
mammal found in Europe.

In order to gather and store 2 lbs. of honey (an average harvest for an average hive on a sunny summer day), 60,000 worker bees visit 3,000,000 flowers in one hour.

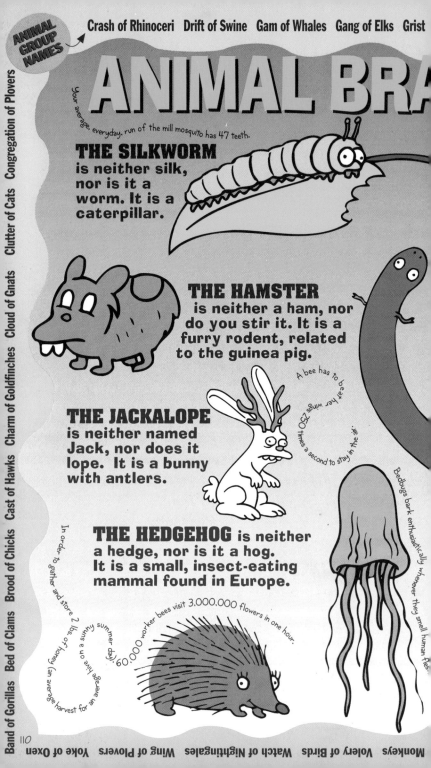

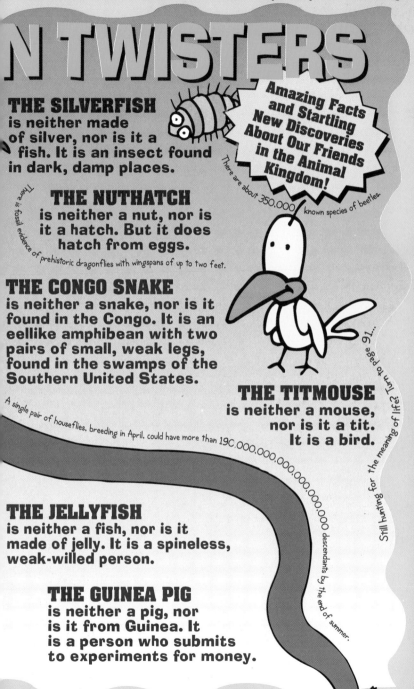

N TWISTERS

Amazing Facts and Startling New Discoveries About Our Friends in the Animal Kingdom!

THE SILVERFISH
is neither made of silver, nor is it a fish. It is an insect found in dark, damp places.

There are about 350,000 known species of beetles.

THE NUTHATCH
is neither a nut, nor is it a hatch. But it does hatch from eggs.

There is fossil evidence of prehistoric dragonflies with wingspans of up to two feet.

THE CONGO SNAKE
is neither a snake, nor is it found in the Congo. It is an eellike amphibean with two pairs of small, weak legs, found in the swamps of the Southern United States.

THE TITMOUSE
is neither a mouse, nor is it a tit. It is a bird.

A single pair of houseflies, breeding in April, could have more than 190,000,000,000,000,000,000 descendants by the end of summer.

Still hunting for the meaning of life? Turn to page 91...

THE JELLYFISH
is neither a fish, nor is it made of jelly. It is a spineless, weak-willed person.

THE GUINEA PIG
is neither a pig, nor is it from Guinea. It is a person who submits to experiments for money.

s.e.x.

8

Most Disgusting Love Songs of All Time:

1 MY EARS GET SWEATY (WHEN YOU PASS MY WAY)
~ Frenchy McPhee

2 I'D EAT A BARREL OF LIVER 'N' ONIONS FOR YOUR LOVE
~ Ding & the Dongs

3 POOPSIE! POOPSIE! POOPSIE!
~ Guy Trembell and his Polka Rangers

4 SLICE MY HEART INTO A HUNDRED PIECES AND SERVE IT UP WITH SECRET SAUCE
~ Lurleen Lumpkin

5 WUV ME OR WEAVE ME
~ Ooh La La Bink

6 TRY ME ON FOR THIGHS
~ Kareem and Jenny

7 I THINK YOU NEED A MASSAGE
~ Bucketful O' Funk

8 IF YOU EVER LEAVE ME I WILL HUNT YOU DOWN AND KILL YOU
~ Rash

TRADITIONAL GRADE-SCHOO LOVE CHANTS

LISA AND MARTIN, SITTIN' IN A TREE, K - I - S - S - I - N - G. FIRST COMES LOVE, THEN COMES MARRIAGE, THEN COMES LISA PUSHIN' A BABY CARRIAGE!

(The Naughty Version!)

I SEE PARIS, I SEE FRANCE, I SEE (your love object's name here) 'S UNDERPANTS!

TEACHER, TEACHER, I DECLARE I SEE (your love object's name here) 'S BOTTOM BARE!

GRADE-SC

A GUIDE TO LOVE FO

Cherished Mementos

(The lovesick grade-schoolers' most prized possessions)

♥ The bruise on my arm from where she punched me.

♥ The lock of hair I yanked out of her head.

♥ The spit-wad she shot at me.

♥ The death threat she sent me.

♥ The black eye she gave me.

♥ The permanent scar she gave me, which I will cherish for the rest of my life.

SHE MUST REALLY LOVE ME!

WARNING SIGNS

How to tell if someone likes you!

They:
- ♥ Chase you around the schoolyard.
- ♥ Giggle annoyingly every time you see them.
- ♥ Make fun of you.
- ♥ Ignore you.
- ♥ Call your house and hang up when you answer the phone.
- ♥ Insult you.

What to do:

Don't panic. Remain calm. The less you react, the more agitated they become. So stay cool!

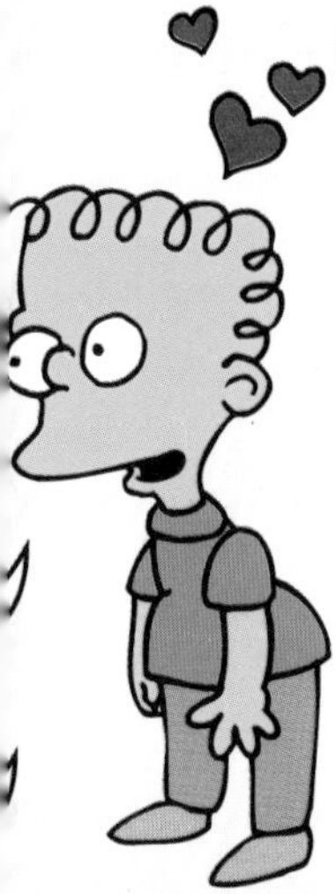

HOOL ROMANCE

HE BEFUDDLED ADOLESCENT

THE LANGUAGE OF L♥VE

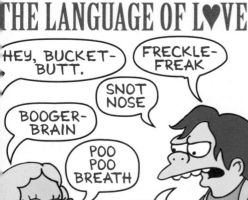

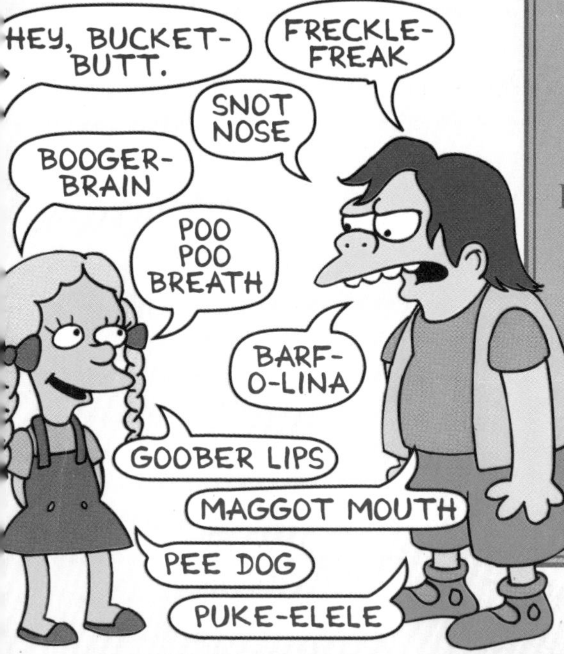

HEY, BUCKET-BUTT.
FRECKLE-FREAK
SNOT NOSE
BOOGER-BRAIN
POO POO BREATH
BARF-O-LINA
GOOBER LIPS
MAGGOT MOUTH
PEE DOG
PUKE-ELELE

Remember the age-old grade-school romance conundrum:

HATE = LOVE

The more they act like they hate you, the more they really like you!*

*Unless, of course they really hate you.

BART AND LISA'S TOP 1

GIRLS

FRUIT TOOTY

1. They smell like fruity chewing gum.

2. They never wanna play rough.

3. Their stupid, girlish, behind-your-back rudeness.

4. Their brainless giggling.

5. They sling mud about each other.

6. They act so smart just to get attention.

7. They say things just to see what effect it ha upon impact.

8. They never stop combing their hair.

GRRR!

9. They are soooo cruel.

10. We have nothing in common with one another.

RECONCEIVED NOTIONS ABOUT

AND BOYS

. They reek of
orn nuts and sweat.

. They always
anna play rough.

3. Their
dumb,
macho,
n-your-face
rudeness.

4. Their idiotic guffawing.

5. They hurl dirt clods
at each other.

6. They act
real dumb
just to get
attention.

7. They throw
hings just to see what
ffect it has upon impact.

3. They
never comb
their hair.

GRRR!

9. They are soooo mean.

10. We have nothing in
common with one another.

BABIES: WHERE

Everyone digs cute little babies, right? But from whence do these bite-size bundles of squealing humanoid flesh originate? Our man-on-the-street, Bartholomew J. (for "jestation") Simpson, put the question to some of Springfield's finest. Here are the answers we got.

MARGE SIMPSON
"Um...wait 'til your father gets home and he'll explain it to you."

JANEY POWELL
"I think the milkman brings them."

MILHOUSE VAN HOUTEN
"They're made at the North Pole by happy little elves."

LEWIS
"You call up and order one just like a pizza, only it takes nine months for delivery. But if they deliver it late, the baby's free."

EDNA KRABAPPEL
"Shiftless husbands give them to their young and nubile secretaries. The best years of my life down the toilet and now he's playing house with that bimbo from the typing pool. There, are you satisfied?"

RALPH WIGGUM
"My parents said they got me through a mail-order catalog."

TODD FLANDERS
"I'm not sure exactly, but you can go to Hell for asking that question."

GROUNDSKEEPER WILLIE
"Laddie, ask me again and you'll be conducting yer w survey from the bottom c a well."

BARNEY GUMBEL
"Oh my God! Am I pregna again?!"

MOE
"Don't worry, Barney. I'l make an honest man out c you."

LISA SIMPSON
"All I know is, you were t result of a biogenetic experiment gone awry. Bu Mom and Dad swore me t secrecy, so if you ask the they'll deny it."

...ROM THEY COME?

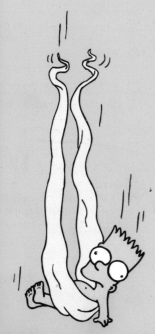

KRUSTY THE CLOWN
"Due to the voluminous amount of mail that Krusty receives, he is unable to answer your question. Keep watchin', kids!"

SIDESHOW MEL
No answer/Honking noises

NELSON MUNTZ
"From the looks of you I'd say the zoo. Haw haw!"

JASPER
"Scabies?! Dagnabbit, you can tell?!!"

KENT BROCKMAN
"Babies? Babies. . . let's see. . . hmmm. . . why don't you go ask that college intern over there?"

GRAMPA SIMPSON
"Rabies?!! Here--put this mustard plaster on your chest and you'll feel better in no time."

SHERRI AND TERRI
"Duh! Everybody knows the stork drops them down your chimney!"

HOMER SIMPSON
"Go ask your mother."

Psychology

WHAT THE HATS ARE SAYING:

HAIR NET
-- Hair is a valuable thing that must be protected at all cost.

SHOWER CAP
-- It keeps the aliens from controlling my mind.

JESTER'S HAT
--I was just kidding when I called you Old Yeller.

BERET
-- I hand-roll my cigarettes.

LAMPSHADE
--Pour me another li'l drinkie an' I'll show you my famous moonwalk.

COWBOY HAT
--I'm a rugged individualist, just like everyone else.

CHEF'S HAT
--Drag. I burned the corndogs again.

SOMBRERO
-- Where did my date go?

WHAT THE HANDS ARE SAYING:

ACTION	MEANING
Fingers drumming ceaselessly.	Your actions are beginning to irritate me just a teensy bit.
Fingers massaging the temples.	I am afraid that your youthful exuberance is getting the better of me.
Hands pressed together as in prayer.	I beg of you, stop that racket this instant or I may need to take further action.
Hands made into fists.	I am feeling very tense now and may soon be unable to contain my anger.
Knuckles turn whitish in color	I sense my blood pressure rising rapidly.
Hands around your neck.	I am unhappy with your behavior and feel I must take corrective action.

Still confused? Learn what life really means by turning to page 20...

RAGED   IRATE   INCENSED   FURIOUS   MADDENED   VEXED   INDIGNANT   HUNGRY

HONEST-TO-GOD PHOBIAS

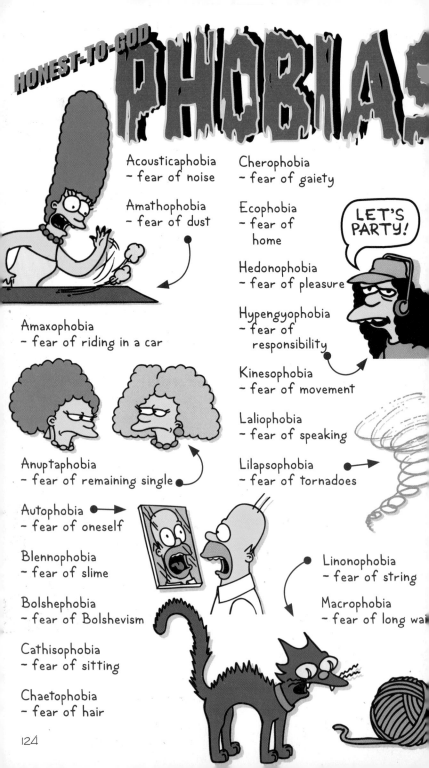

Acousticaphobia
– fear of noise

Amathophobia
– fear of dust

Amaxophobia
– fear of riding in a car

Anuptaphobia
– fear of remaining single

Autophobia
– fear of oneself

Blennophobia
– fear of slime

Bolshephobia
– fear of Bolshevism

Cathisophobia
– fear of sitting

Chaetophobia
– fear of hair

Cherophobia
– fear of gaiety

Ecophobia
– fear of home

Hedonophobia
– fear of pleasure

Hypengyophobia
– fear of responsibility

Kinesophobia
– fear of movement

Laliophobia
– fear of speaking

Lilapsophobia
– fear of tornadoes

Linonophobia
– fear of string

Macrophobia
– fear of long wai

LET'S PARTY!

Megalophobia
– fear of large things

Melissophobia
– fear of bees

Metrophobia
– fear of poetry

Nebulaphobia
– fear of fog

Papaphobia
– fear of
   the Pope

Philophobia
– fear of
   falling in love

Placeophobia
– fear of
   tombstones

Pogonophobia
– fear of beards

Poloticophobia
– fear of politicians

Pteronophobia
– fear of
   being
   tickled by
   feathers

Rhytiphobia
– fear of
   getting
   wrinkles

Septophobia
– fear of decaying matter

Soceraphobia
– fear of parents-in-law

Sophophobia
– fear of learning

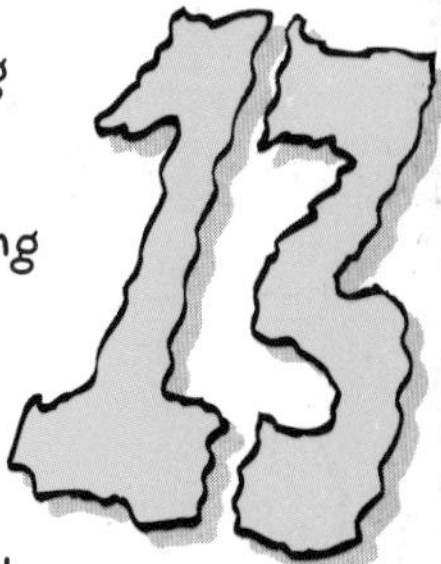

Stasibasiphobia
– fear of standing

Stygiophobia
– fear of Hell

Tapinophobia
– fear of small things

Technophobia
– fear of arts and crafts

Triskadekaphobia
– fear of the number
   thirteen

Uranophobia
– fear of Heaven

Verbophobia
– fear of words

Xylophobia
– fear of wooden things

Pantophobia
– fear of everything

Phobophobia
– fear of fear itself

125

Putting Your **PHOB**

Pay attention, now. Fear can b
put to good use, man. You
can get out of doing just abou
anything by using the
following clinically proven
technique, courtesy of
Dr. Bartholomew J. Simpseür

Napoleon suffered from aelurophobia, or the fear of cats.

Degas became nauseous whenever in the presence of flowers or perfume.

Just string some Greek root-words together
and stick "phobia" at the end. Tired of eating
organ meats for dinner? No problem . . .

Thomas Hobbes feared the dark and always slept with the lights on.

> SORRY, MOM. I'VE GOT
> PHAGOHEPAROPHOBIA.
> NO LIVER FOR ME EVER AGAIN.

or

> I'D REALLY LOVE TO KISS
> YOU, AUNT SELMA, BUT
> I'VE GOT LIPORHINOPHOBIA.

or the best one of all

> GOSH, MISS KRABAPPEL,
> IF IT WASN'T FOR MY
> SCRIPTERGOPHOBIA I'D HAVE
> ALL MY REPORTS IN ON TIME!

Winston Churchill had a neat trick to help him overcome his stage fright. He would imagine that every person in his audience had a hole in their sock.

cacoerophobia – fear of bad breath, hypnotopophobia – fear of making your bed, gymnogasterophobia – fear of naked bellies,

The 6 Phobic Signs:
1. Rapid pulse rate 2. Sweating palms
3. Rapid breathing 4. Raised blood pressure
5. Increased muscle tension 6. Wet pants

Now you try. Match up some of the words below
and see what they can do for you.

Greek – English

aero – air	gluco – sweet	phono – voice, sound
amatho – dust	gymn – naked	ploss – tongue
anemo – wind	hagio – holy	presby – old
athlet – contest	hepar – liver	psycho – spirit, mind
biblio – book	herp – to creep	rhino – nose
caco – bad	hygro – wet	sauro – lizard
chaeto – hair	hypno – sleep	scop – look at, view
cholero – anger	kara – head	script – to write
choreo – dancing	lalia – talk	skelet – dry, hard
copro – dung	latr – worship	sphaira – ball
derma – skin	lep – scaly	tacho – quick
didacto – to teach	lipo – fat	taph – burial
dys – badly, ill	myco – fungus	tempo – time
eco – house	odonto – tooth	thana – death
emet – to vomit	oion – egg	topo – place
ergo – work	orat – to speak	tribo – to rub
eroto – sexual love, desire	oxy – sharp	uro – urine
galacto – milk	pater – father	xeno – guest, stranger
gastero – stomach	phago – to eat	
	philo – to love	

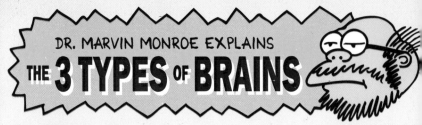

DR. MARVIN MONROE EXPLAINS
THE 3 TYPES OF BRAINS

You know, like the earth, your brain is divided into two hemispheres – a right one and a left one. And, for most people, one hemisphere is more dominant, or controlling, than the other. And this is what often determines a person's personality traits, talents, abilities and way of thinking. . . unless, of course, that person has Brain Type #3. This is a brain in which neither hemisphere wishes to be involved in determining traits, talents, abilities, or even day-to-day decisions.

#1 THE LEFT-BRAINER

Meticulous, fussy, petty & uptight. Often these persons become bean counters, computer nerds or IRS agents.

#2 THE RIGHT-BRAINER

Self-absorbed, artsy-fartsy & flaky. Often these types become artists, poets, cartoonists, or street mimes.

#3 THE NO-BRAINER

Stupid, mindless & happy-go-lucky. Often they become politicians, models and sit-com writers.

128

129

Law & Order

Real LAWS OF THE LAND

WILBUR, WA
You can be fined $300 for riding an ugly horse.

GARFIELD COUNTY, MT
You are not allowed to draw funny faces on your window shades.

NORTH DAKOTA
It's illegal to fall asleep with your shoes on.

PORTLAND, OR
You can get busted for taking a bath without wearing suitable clothing.

HOOD RIVER, OR
The police won't let you juggle without a juggling license.

MONTANA
It's a felony for a wife to open her husband's mail.

BELVEDERE, CA
A dog can't be in a public place without its master on a leash.

WATERLOO, NE
Barbers may not eat onions between the hours of 7 A.M. and 7 P.M.

SAN FRANCISCO, CA
It's illegal to spray people's clothing with saliva spewed out of your mouth.

NEVADA
It's illegal to drive down a public highway on a camel.

YUKON, OK
Patients are not allowed to pull their dentist's teeth.

CALIFORNIA
It's illegal to duck hunt while flying in an airplane.

NORMAL, OK
It's illegal to make an ugly face at a dog.

LOS ANGELES, CA
You can't bathe two babies in the same tub at the same time.

CARRIZOZO, NM
Women can't be caught unshaven in public.

FAIRBANKS, AK
They'll put you in jail for serving alcoholic beverages to a moose.

HAWAII
It's all right to compete in a swim meet just as long as you don't wear swim trunks.

136

MAN!

Forget all that baloney they try to teach you in school. This ain't a free country, bub, especially when the cops are around. If you don't believe me, just try taking your yo-yo out for a spin the next time you're in Memphis on a Sunday. If you do get caught with your pants down, follow these 3 simple rules: I didn't do it. Nobody saw me do it. You can't prove anything. If that doesn't work, plead insanity. I'll back you 100 percent, man.

INTERNATIONAL FALLS, MN
It's against the law for cats to chase dogs up telephone poles.

ROCHESTER, NY
Kids are not allowed to collect old cigar stubs as a hobby.

NEW HAMPSHIRE
It's against the law to dye margarine pink.

MICHIGAN
A woman's hair is owned exclusively by her husband.

CONNECTICUT
You could go to jail for trying to educate a dog.

HOMER, IL
Only police officers can legally carry slingshots.

SOUTH BEND, IN
It's against the law for monkeys to smoke cigarettes.

PENNSYLVANIA
It's against the law for babysitters to raid refrigerators.

MARYLAND
It's illegal to take a lion to the movies.

ELKHART, IN
Barbers are prohibited from scaring children into being quiet by threatening to cut off their ears.

TENNESSEE
You're forbidden to use a lasso to catch fish.

VIRGINIA
It's illegal to take a bath without a doctor's permission.

BOO.

SACO, MO
It's against the law for women to wear hats that might frighten children or animals.

NATCHEZ, MS
It's illegal for an elephant to guzzle a beer.

MIAMI, FL
Men are strictly forbidden to wear strapless gowns in public.

HOUSTON, TX
You are not allowed to buy Limburger cheese, goose liver, or rye bread on a Sunday.

SARASOTA, FL
Don't get caught singing in a bikini, or you'll be singing the blues in jail.

WANTED

Turn to page 82 to reveal the secret meaning of life...

Xmas

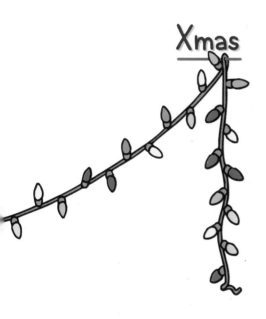

THE CASE FOR

We see him on TV.

Millions of people can't be wrong.

Catchy Christmas jingles.

Presents under the tree.

Xmas specials.

Milk & cookies gone in morning.

He's part of our rich cultural tradition.

The North Pole is included on most official maps.

Stranger things have happened.

Elves.

Our parents wouldn't lie to us.

HELLO AGAIN, MY GULLIBLE FRIENDS. THIS HERE IS THE PART OF THE BOOK WHERE WE DEBATE THE TIMEWORN QUESTION: IS SANTA CLAUS FOR REAL OR JUST A FIGMENT OF THE DERANGED IMAGINATIONS OF ADVERTISERS AND TV PRODUCERS? YOU BE THE JUDGE, MAN.

IS SANT

UNDER-ACHIEVERS ANONYMOUS GIVE

140

A REAL?

THE CASE AGAINST

We see him riding shavers.

People will believe anything.

How come you get presents even when you're bad?

Why does Santa give rich people more toys than poor people?

Xmas commercials.

Kisses under the mistletoe.

He's the embodiment of crass consumerism.

Who the hell would choose to live at the North Pole?

How does a stranger know your shoe size?

Elves.

Grow up, man.

OF COURSE, IF YOU DECIDE THAT THIS SANTA THING IS ONE BIG HOAX, AND THEN ALL YOU GET FOR CHRISTMAS NEXT YEAR IS A LUMP OF COAL, DON'T COME CRYING TO ME!

THE 12 DAYS OF XMAS

On the **1st** day of Xmas this cool guy gave to me **SOME BONGOS WITH A GOATEE**.

On the **2nd** day of Xmas this cool guy gave to me **TWO MONSTER TRUCKS** and some bongos with a goatee.

On the **3rd** day of Xmas this cool guy gave to me **THREE SKATEBOARDS**, two monster trucks and some bongos with a goatee.

On the **4th** day of Xmas this cool guy gave to me **FOUR KRUSTY DOLLS**, three skateboards, two monster trucks and some bongos with a goatee.

On the **5th** day of Xmas this cool guy gave to me **FIVE RUDE TATTOOS**, four Krusty dolls, three skateboards, two monster trucks and some bongos with a goatee.

On the **6th** day of Xmas this cool guy gave to me **SIX COSMIC DEATH RAYS**, FIVE RUDE TATTOOS, four Krusty dolls, three skateboards, two monster trucks and some bongos with a goatee.

On the **7th** day of Xmas this cool guy gave to me **SEVEN BOOTLEG T-SHIRTS**, six cosmic death rays, FIVE RUDE TATTOOS, four Krusty dolls, three skateboards, two monster trucks and some bongos with a goatee.

...If you still want to know the meaning of life, turn to page 23

144

On the **8th** day of Xmas
this cool guy gave to me
EIGHT JUMBO SQUISHEES,
seven bootleg T-shirts, six cosmic
death rays, FIVE RUDE TATTOOS, four
Krusty dolls, three skateboards, two
monster trucks and some bongos with
a goatee.

On the **9th** day of Xmas
this cool guy gave to me
NINE TOADS A-LEAPING,
eight jumbo Squishees, seven bootleg
T-shirts, six cosmic death rays, FIVE
RUDE TATTOOS, four Krusty dolls, three
skateboards, two monster trucks and
some bongos with a goatee.

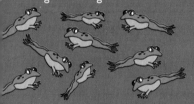

On the **10th** day of Xmas
this cool guy gave to me
TEN COBRAS SPITTING, nine
toads a-leaping, eight jumbo
Squishees, seven bootleg T-shirts, six
cosmic death rays, FIVE RUDE
TATTOOS, four Krusty dolls, three
skateboards, two monster trucks and
some bongos with a goatee.

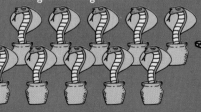

On the **11th** day of Xmas
this cool guy gave to me
**ELEVEN ZOMBIES
LURCHING**, ten cobras spitting,
nine toads a-leaping, eight jumbo
Squishees, seven bootleg T-shirts, six
cosmic death rays, FIVE RUDE
TATTOOS, four Krusty dolls, three
skateboards, two monster trucks and
some bongos with a goatee.

On the **12th** day of Xmas
this cool guy gave to me
**TWELVE MILLION
DOLLARS**, eleven zombies lurching,
ten cobras spitting, nine toads
a-leaping, eight jumbo Squishees, seven
bootleg T-shirts, six cosmic death rays,
FIVE RUDE TATTOOS, four Krusty dolls,
three skateboards, two monster trucks
and some bongos with a goatee.

DECORATE YOUR FATHER'S BELLY
(Sung to the tune of "Deck the Halls")

Decorate your father's belly,
 Fa la la la la, la la la la,
While he's sleeping by the telly,
 Fa la la la la, la la la la.
Jelly smeared in patterns festive,
 Fa la la, la la la, la la la,
Makes a centerpiece suggestive,
 Fa la la la la, la la la la.

Next create a yuletide bonbon,
 Fa la la la la, la la la la,
Drip some chocolate sauce upon him,
 Fa la la la la, la la la la.
Better chase away the pets now,
 Fa la la, la la la, la la la,
Or your dad is X-mas dog chow,
 Fa la la la la, la la la la.

Colored lights his belly wreathing,
 Fa la la la la, la la la la,
Blend so gaily with his breathing,
 Fa la la la la, la la la la.
Crowning all, a star above it,
 Fa la la, la la la, la la la.
Show the neighbors, they will love it,
 Fa la la la la, la la la la.

If your dad begins to waken,
 Fa la la la la, la la la la,
Hide the tinsel-covered bacon,
 Fa la la la la, la la la la.
Tell him that he looks delicious,
 Fa la la, la la la , la la la,
Run like hell, he might get vicious,
 Fa la la la la, la la la la.

O CANNIBALS, O CANNIBALS
(Sung to the tune of "O Christmas Tree")

O Cannibals, O Cannibals,
What will you eat for Christmas?
O Cannibals, O Cannibals,
What will you eat for Christmas?
Dear Auntie stuffed would be divine,
But then on what would Auntie dine?
O Cannibals, O Cannibals,
What will you eat for Christmas?

O Cannibals, O Cannibals,
You start to make me nervous.
O Cannibals, O Cannibals,
You start to make me nervous.

Your friendly looks
Have turned to smiles,
Reminding me of crocodiles.
O Cannibals, O Cannibals,
You start to make me nervous.

O Cannibals, O Cannibals,
I wish I'd never met you.
O Cannibals, O Cannibals,
I wish I'd never met you.
I hope that when you've eaten me,
I make you barf your recipe.
O Cannibals, O Cannibals,
I wish I'd never met you.

FLAKEY THE LEPER
(Sung to the tune of
"Frosty the Snowman")

Flakey the Leper
Didn't even have a nose.
But he jumped about
With a laugh and shout,
Cause he still had seven toes.

He pranced around the snowy ground
And once he tried to fly
But when he jumped off of the stump
Out dropped his only eye.

Flakey the Leper
Could dance a merry jig.
If you wanted some
Out his hair would come
And you'd have a little wig.

He once came down into our town
Leaning upon his staff

> TIRED OF THE SAME OLD WORDS? TRY THESE ANNOYING AND IMMATURE VARIATIONS.

Xmas Songs to Get You through the Holidays.

And when his ear
Fell in some beer
He made us
Start to laugh.

Flakey the Leper
Was a jolly, jolly sort.
Even though his legs
Were attached with pegs
He remained a real good sport.

We all can learn a lesson
From Flakey's carefree pranks.
If ever bad luck comes our way
We should merely answer "Thanks!"

Soooooooo,
Flakey the Leper
In his smile resides his grace.
For even though
He's beset with woe
He has never yet lost face.

147

Strange Facts

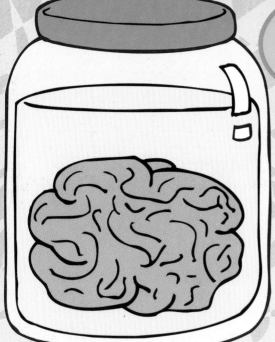

How can we know for sure we're not dreaming all this, and that actually we're just a brain in a jar in some mad scientist's laboratory?

What if we think the joke's on them, but the joke is really on us?

If Heaven is so great for everybody, then wh scrubs the toilets up there?

Is there yodeling in Hell?

Why isn't creamed cor against the law?

Everyone knows that Secret Sauce is just sugar, mayonnaise, salt, and . . . what? What is that tantalizing, mouth-watering, mystery flavor?

Why are movie sequels always so bad, yet so irresistible?

How do we know that the entire universe isn't just the fleeting daydream of a magic super-beetle in some parallel world?

What if God doesn't really dig my youthful high jinks?

YSTERIES

N I CAN'T EXPLAIN

Why did God create
dung beetles?

Is there Secret Sauce
in Heaven?

Wouldn't the world
be a happier place
if everyone would
just strut around
nude?

If you want to know what the meaning of life is, turn to page 110...

Why did God create tapeworms?

Does God like Secret Sauce?

Why did God create Barney the Dinosaur?

Isn't the ultimate answer to any question, no matter how profound,
thoughtful, or cosmic, merely "Who cares?"

If God can do
anything, could He
drink so much
Secret Sauce that
He'd get sick to
His stomach?

When the Three Little Pigs kept saying.
"Not by the hair on my chinny-chin-chin," what
the hell were they talking about?

153

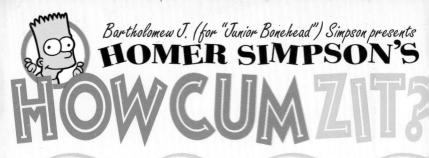

Bartholomew J. (for "Junior Bonehead") Simpson presents

HOMER SIMPSON'S
HOW CUM ZIT?

HOW COME they don't make a perfume that smells like dough frying?

EAU DE DOUGH

HOW COME they call it a "winter wonderland" when there's just a bunch of freezing snow and ice all over the place?

HOW COME you can't drive golf carts on the freeway?

HOW COME someone with as little hair as me has so much head lice?

HOW COME corndogs are so magically delicious?

HOW COME you have to buy a whole entire snow-cone when all you really want is the sweet, sweet syrup flavoring?

HOW COME I sweat when I e...

HOW COME women don't realize that baldness is sexy?

154

HOW COME the guy who invented the hammock isn't considered to be the greatest genius who ever lived?

HOW COME two wrongs don't make a right, no matter how hard I try?

HOW COME cats think they're so smart with their fancy footwork and their crafty schemes to eat all my smelts?

HOW COME stamp glue tastes so magically delicious?

HOW COME they don't have super comfy soft vibrating couches for bowling alleys, so you can lie down when you're waiting for your next turn?

HOW COME people say that TV is a dull and stupefying waste of time with no real benefit to humanity when there's so much fine entertainment on 24 hours a day?

HOW COME Marge leaves that baking soda box open in the back of the refrigerator, and when I try to eat it, it tastes really funny?

HOW COME they don't serve the second greatest beverage – I'm referring, of course, to eggnog – all year long?

HOW COME I'm cursed with a son who is always plotting against me no matter how often I let him polish my bowling trophies?

HOW COME there is really only one thing in the universe that's interesting and that's food?

THE WONDERFUL V

1. THE DEADLY MANTIS
2. BIGFOOT (Sasquatch)
3. THE BLOB
4. THE 50 FT. WOMAN
5. THE LEPUS
6. GIANT SQUID
7. THE JOLLY GREEN GIANT
8. COLOSSAL MAN
9. ZOMBIES (The Living Dead)
10. THEM

11. WORLD'S LARGEST PEANUT
12. KING KONG
13. SNOWBALL, THE KILLER GOAT
14. THE CREATURE FROM THE
    BLACK LAGOON
15. THE THING
16. THE LOCH NESS MONSTER
17. MR. HYDE
18. JAWS
19. MONSTRO
20. THE WEREWOLF
21. THE INVISIBLE MAN

RLD OF MONSTERS

22. THE HUNCHBACK OF NOTRE DAME
23. THE PHANTOM OF THE OPERA
24. MEDUSA
25. SPACE MUTANTS
26. FRANKENSTEIN'S MONSTER
27. COUNT DRACULA
28. THE GOLEM
29. THE CYCLOPS
30. THE MUMMY
31. BRIDE OF FRANKENSTEIN
32. CECIL THE SEASICK SEA SERPENT
33. GHIDRAH
34. THE TRIFFIDS
35. YETI (Abominable Snowman)
36. MOBY DICK
37. MINYA (Tadzilla)
38. GODZILLA
39. GIANT CLAM
40. GIANT OCTOPUS
41. TASMANIAN DEVIL

157

MONSTERS MAD[E]

NAME	HABITAT OR PLACE OF ORIGIN	TRAITS
1. THE DEADLY MANTIS	The Arctic/ Migrates to Washington, D.C.	[Menace to Humanity] [Giant]
2. BIGFOOT (Sasquatch)	Northwestern United States and Canada	[?]
3. THE BLOB	Meteor/ Lands in unnamed small town in U.S.	[= blob] [Shape-changer] [Menace to Humanity]
4. THE 50 FT. WOMAN	Somewhere in California	[Giant] [Ø] [Man-made/atom]
5. THE LEPUS	Arizona	[Flesh-eater] [Shape-changer] [Giant]
6. GIANT SQUID	20,000 leagues beneath the sea	[Aquatic Creature] [Giant]
7. THE JOLLY GREEN GIANT	The Valley of the Jolly Green Giant	[Giant] [TV]
8. COLOSSAL MAN	Southwest U.S. and Mexico	[Giant] [Man-made/atom]
9. ZOMBIES (The Living Dead)	Southeastern U.S. and Caribbean	[Man-made] [Menace to Humanity] [Flesh-eater]
10. THEM	New Mexico/ The sewers of Los Angeles	[Man-made/atom] [Menace to Humanity] [Giant]
11. WORLD'S LARGEST PEANUT	Ashburn, Georgia	[Giant]
12. KING KONG	Skull Island/Later shipped to Manhattan	[Giant] [Shape-changer] [Ø]
13. SNOWBALL, THE KILLER GOAT	Locust Grove, Georgia	[Shape-changer]
14. THE CREATURE FROM THE BLACK LAGOON	The Black Lagoon, in the upper reaches of the Amazon	[creature] [Ø] [Aquatic Creature]
15. THE THING	Outer space/ Lands in the Arctic	[Shape-changer] [= blob]
16. THE LOCH NESS MONSTER	Loch Ness, Scotland	[creature] [?] [Aquatic Creature]
17. MR. HYDE	London, England	[Shape-changer]
18. JAWS	The Atlantic Ocean, primarily	[Aquatic Creature] [Flesh-eater]
19. MONSTRO	The Seven Seas	[Aquatic Creature]
20. THE WEREWOLF	London, England	[Shape-changer]

LEGEND

	Flesh-eater [icon]	Man-made [icon]
Aquatic Creature [icon]	Giant [icon]	Shape-changer [icon]
Mythical Beast [icon]	Blood-drinker [icon]	Menace to Humanity [icon]

IN HANDY, BEAST-O-MATIC, POCKET-SIZE GUIDE FORM!

MWAHA HAHAHA HAHA!!!

NAME	HABITAT OR PLACE OF ORIGIN	TRAITS
1. THE INVISIBLE MAN	London, England	🧍 🚫
2. THE HUNCHBACK OF NOTRE DAME	Paris, France	🚫 ?
3. THE PHANTOM OF THE OPERA	Paris, France	🚫 ?
4. MEDUSA	An island somewhere in Asia Minor	🐎
5. SPACE MUTANTS	Outer space	🛸 🌐
6. FRANKENSTEIN'S MONSTER	Geneva, Switzerland	⚡ 🚫
7. COUNT DRACULA	Transylvania, Romania	🦇
8. THE GOLEM	Prague, Czechoslovakia	✝ ⚡ 🌐
9. THE CYCLOPS	Colossa Island	🐎
0. THE MUMMY	Cairo, Egypt	⚰
1. BRIDE OF FRANKENSTEIN	Geneva, Switzerland	⚡
2. CECIL THE SEASICK SEA SERPENT	Unknown	🐟 📺
3. GHIDRAH	Japan, by way of Mars	🛸 🌐
4. THE TRIFFIDS	The former Soviet Union	⚡ 🌐
5. YETI (Abominable Snowman)	The Himalayas	?
6. MOBY DICK	The Seven Seas	🐟 🦠
7. MINYA (Tadzilla)	Sol-Gell Island in the South Seas	🐊
8. GODZILLA	Comes to Tokyo via Oto Island	🐊
9. GIANT CLAM	The ocean floor	🐟 🧍 ⊠
0. GIANT OCTOPUS	The ocean	🐟 🧍
1. TASMANIAN DEVIL	Tasmania, Australia	🦠 📺

Misunderstood Social Outcast 🚫   Space Alien 🛸   Overgrown Reptile 🐊

Recluse ?   Immortal Being/Undead ⚰   Psychotic Mammal 🦠

See-thru 🧍   Nuclear Radiation Mutation ⚛   TV Personality 📺

...you know what to look for. Just follow this simple guide and you'll be able to identify a space mutant a block away. Bone up now! The future of planet Earth is depending on you, man.

NEWSPRINT STAINS ON FINGERS

From cheap supermarket tabloids, the aliens' main source for news of his extraterrestrial brothers and hometown gossip.

BAGGY PANTS

Aside from the head and hands, alien anatomy is hideously different from ours and must be concealed.

DACRON SOCKS

A mysterious fabric from the planet Mun-Dan. (Note: Although alien in origin, Dacron has been adopted by earthlings too. Check your dad's closet for examples.)

MYSTERIOUS SPOT ON TIE

Probably from most recent human sacrifice.

ROTARIANS TIE TACK

Really a cleverly concealed micro-death ray. Anyone seen wearing one of these is definitely an alien and should be reported to the authorities. Note: Many authority figures are, in actuality, aliens themselves, so beware.

FEET

Nerveless and extremely hard. More than a visual ID is required here. Just stomp on the feet in question as hard as you can. If it's an alien, it won't feel a thing. If it's human, be prepared to run like hell.

160

ALIENS
THEY WALK AMONG US!

ALIENS. NOT THE ILLEGAL KIND. THE HIDEOUS MUTATIONS FROM OUTER SPACE KIND, MAN. THEY'RE ALL AROUND US. TO THE CASUAL OBSERVER, THEY MAY SEEM LIKE NORMAL HUMAN BEINGS, BUT

BAGS UNDER THE EYES
Actually scars from surgical removal of third and fourth eyes.

RIGID POSTURE
Try as they may, aliens have yet to master the perfect slouch.

DRAB ATTIRE
Must be worn by alien at all times. Bright colors interfere with the Zigma waves being beamed to them from the mother ship. Without these beams they would surely die.

DORKY HAIRSTYLE
Many aliens wear telltale removable hairpieces. Actually not hair at all, these densely woven networks of transmission fibers enable the alien to communicate with central command. Often detectable in high winds.

VACANT STARE
Noticeable when alien is receiving mental directives from the Supreme Commander.

INCESSANT SCOWL
Caused by their digestive systems' inability to handle our rude food, dude.

OUTMODED LANGUAGE
Adapted from ancient TV transmissions that aliens have intercepted in space, decades

NOW JUST A DARN TOOTIN' MINUTE, SON!

161

Now that you've spotted your alien, you'll need proof positive that your subject is indeed of the mutation persuasion. Here are more things to look for:

ALIEN

ZIPPERATIC CHECKIFICATION

Upon exiting any rest room, the male alien will automatically check his fly. This is a form of salute to the Supreme Commander who is always watching. (The female counterpart to this tribute is a quick tug on the skirt or panty hose.)

ELEVATORIAL ZOMBIFICATION

In an elevator, the alien will always face front, stare hypnotically at the lighted numbers, and lose the ability to speak.

BEHAVIOR

AUTOMOTIVE EMBARRASSATORY ACTIVITY

When driving cars alone, aliens believe they're invisible to the world outside. Apparently, the windows in their spaceships are made of one-way glass, and they assume that automobile windows are the same. Thus, they take advantage of their perceived privacy by cleaning out their ears and noses, singing loudly, and playing imaginary musical instruments.

CHILD/ANIMAL CONFUSIOTOMY

Aliens can often be seen walking children on leashes and barking commands like "NO!" or "STAY!" On the other hand, they dress their pets in ski sweaters and communicate with them using baby talk. Listen for phrases such as "Momma's little poopsie woopsie" and "See's my widdle baby, yes see is!" This behavior remains unexplained.

RELENTLESS FACIAL INSPECTION

Aliens maintain elaborate disguises in order to walk among humans undetected. The female disguise is more complex than the male, and thus more fragile. A female alien may be seen constantly inspecting and repairing her human veneer. Although seemingly unconcerned with his appearance, the male alien will always do a quick spot-check when passing any reflective surface.

OTHER TELL-TALE WARNING SIGNS

Mustache waxing	Nail biting
Egg sucking	Butt picking
Finger snapping	Knuckle cracking
Boot licking	High fiveing
Leg jiggling	Bird flipping
Foot tapping	Hip wriggling
Grand standing	Lick spittling
One upping	Hair splitting
Finger pointing	Arm twisting
Beard stroking	Brown nosing

Religion

SLOTH

GREED

LUST

GLUTTONY

HELLO THERE, FRIENDS! PLANNING ON A HEAVENLY AFTERLIFE? I WOULDN'T COUNT ON IT IF I WERE YOU. BUT IF YOU SIMPLY MUST KNOW WHAT SORT OF FATE AWAITS YOU IN THE HEREAFTER, JUST TAKE THIS SIMPLE LITTLE QUIZ... SEE YOU 'ROUND!

SLOTH
I like to:
    a. Put off 'til tomorrow what I can do toda
    b. Take an occasional nap on the job.
    c. Hibernate in winter.

GREED
I have:
    a. Left restaurants without tipping.
    b. Left restaurants without paying the chec
    c. Made a killing in cartoon merchandising.

LUST
I am sexually aroused by:
    a. Attractive members of the opposite sex.
    b. Attractive members of the same sex.
    c. Drainpipes.

7 DEADLY SINS

GLUTTONY
I eat:
  a. Between meal snacks.
  b. Between between meal snacks.
  c. Therefore I am.

ENVY
I am jealous of people with:
  a. Good looks.
  b. Hair.
  c. Toupees.

ANGER
I sometimes:
  a. Get "mad."
  b. Get "really mad."
  c. Get my shotgun.

PRIDE
I am:
  a. God's gift to the opposite sex.
  b. God's gift to the world.
  c. God.

How to score
10 points for each a.
20 points for each b.
50 points for each c.

If your total is:
0–70 . . . . you are more than likely going to Hell.
80–150 . . . you are definitely on the road to Hell.
160–350 . . . Hell is your destiny.

ENVY

ANGER

PRIDE

If you are still curious about the meaning of life, turn to page 1...

ZESTY PRAYERS

...FOR ANY AND ALL OCCASIONS!

NATIONAL COUNCIL FOR THE ADVANCEMENT OF MALAPROPISMS · ENDORSED BY THE

SPAM OF GOD

Spam of God,
You spread all over
the buns of the world,
Have mustard on them.

Spam of God,
You spread all over
the buns of the world.
Have mustard on them.

Spam of God
You spread all over
the buns of the world,
Grant us a piece.

PRAYERS - WE ALL NEED 'EM NOW AND THEN: BEFORE A TEST, WHILE BEING CHASED BY HORNETS, IN THE EVENT OF A MELTDOWN AT THE LOCAL NUCLEAR PLANT...
BUT I'M SURE YOU'LL AGREE THEY'RE A TAD ON THE STUFFY SIDE, MAN. SO HERE YOU GO — SOUPED-UP VERSIONS OF ALL YOUR CLASSIC FAVORITES, COURTESY OF HIS HOLIER THAN HOLINESS, BARTHOLOMEW J. (FOR JUDAS) SIMPSON. (REMEMBER: USE SPARINGLY, MAN. GOD HELPS THOSE WHO HELP THEMSELVES.)

HAIL UNDIES

Hail, undies,
plain or lace,
thy loins aren't worthy.
Blessed art thou amongst clothing,
and blessed art thy Fruit of the Looms, all sizes.

Holey undies fall off your bod.
Pray for strong elastic,
now and at the hour of your bath.
Amen.

NOW I LAY ME DOWN TO SLEEP

Now I lay me
down to sleep
I pray my bladder
doesn't leak.
If I should pee
before I wake,
I pray the Lord
to dry my lake.

GOD IS GREAT

God is Great,
God is Good,
Get me through
My Childhood.

MEAL TIME GRACE

Good Food,
Good Drink,
Good God,
Let's Eat!

THE LARDO'S PRAYER

Our Fatty,
Who eats unshaven,
Swallowing is thy game.
Thy Ding Dongs come
Flambéed with some
Liqueur in a red hot oven.
Give up this day your daily bread,
And munch out on watercress,
Or just try to eat less
Trash like donuts!
Lead yourself not
Into temptation,
But eat liver for all meals,
Amen.

ACT OUT CONTRITION

O my God
I am heartily sorry
For having offended You.

But I couldn't help it, man.
It seemed like the
Only thing to do.

OUR
FATHER,
WHO ART IN
HEAVEN,
IS IT
OPEN ALL
NIGHT,
JUST LIKE
7-11?

169

ANNOYING QUESTIONS TO ASK

OTHER USES FOR THIS BOOK

1. Use it to start a fire if your plane goes down in the Andes.
2. Throw it off the Empire State Building and see how big a dent it makes in the sidewalk.
3. Makes a handy coaster for jumbo Squishees!
4. Start a movement to get it banned.
5. Buy a case of them and put them in the trunk of the car to improve traction on snowy days.
6. Tear the pages up into confetti and throw a parade for yourself.
7. Improve your posture by balancing one on your head.
8. Hollow out the center and use it to hide your sensitive poetry.
9. Re-cover it with the jacket of *Quantum Mechanics Made Difficult* and impress your friends.
10. Make spitwads out of the pages.
11. Get three and practice juggling.
12. Use it as a doorstop.
13. Create a little tent for your hamster.
14. Start your own religion and make this your Holy Book.
15. Use it to flatten hamburger into patties.
16. Bequeath it to Brigham Young University.

⚜

INDEX

D

E

SO LONG, SUCKERS

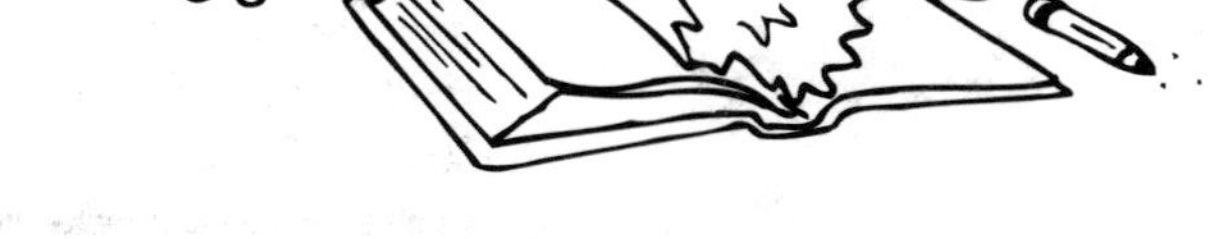